GW00383830

Massimiliano Fuksas. Works and Projects 1970-2005

To Marta

Luca Molinari

Massimiliano Fuksas

Works and Projects 1970-2005

Cover
Detail of the roofing of the
Trade Fair Auditorium, Milan
Photograph by Giuseppe Blencini

Art Director
Marcello Francone

Editing
Elena Bajetta, Marta Cattaneo

Layout
Paola Ranzini

Translations
Leslie Ray, Christopher Evans

First published in Italy in 2005 by
Skira Editore S.p.A.
Palazzo Casati Stampa
via Torino 61
20123 Milano
Italy
www.skira.net

© 2005 by Skira editore

Printed and bound in Italy. First edition

Distributed in North America by Rizzoli International
Publications, Inc., 300 Park Avenue South, New York,
NY 10010.
Distributed elsewhere in the world by Thames and
Hudson Ltd., 181a High Holborn, London WC1V 7QX,
United Kingdom.

Index

Acknowledgements

This work is the result of an initial, unexpected Milan meeting with Massimiliano Fuksas, which progressively became an intense dialogue and then a project. I am an architect who decided some time ago that writing and reflection through the slow daily practice of writing were my way of thinking, making projects and also attempting to contribute to remedying the difficult situation in which architecture finds itself.

All my research arises from the profound love for space, for the civil power that architecture has to build quality and to listen attentively to the reality that is and that will be. In my eclectic paths, I have always attempted to understand and render evident the complexity that architecture produces and administers and I hope this work will also succeed at least partly in this mission.

The construction of a book reproduces on a smaller scale the dimension of dialogue and of constant comparison that is also found in an architectural project and without which architecture could not be realised.

I therefore wish to thank Massimiliano Fuksas for having prompted me to tackle this work and for the continuous, friendly support and advice that, with Doriana Mandrelli, have never been lacking in this year of research and writing.

The Fuksas studio in Rome, as well as the site office at the Rho-Pero Fair, have never failed to be willing to provide assistance and help, and for this I am grateful to the secretarial office and to the Press office.

In this long period of trips and archive research, the assistance, the editing work and the selection of materials carried out by Annaluigia De Simone has been fundamental; she has been an indispensable assistant and a generous friend for the time and energies she has devoted to this work.

In this volume I wanted some significant voices of key clients in Fuksas' recent work to appear, to give account of that necessary dialogue that must always exist between the designer and those who invest financial and human energies to permit an architecture of quality; I therefore very much wish to thank Walter Veltroni, Giorgio Armani, Cristina and Giuseppe Nardini for their patient helpfulness and Mario Cutuli for the Municipality of Rome, Michele Tacchella and the Press office for Giorgio Armani and the Press office for Nardini for enabling me to achieve these results.

Every work slowly takes shape also through the impromptu and disorderly dialogues with the dear friends who have often supported and tolerated my loud ravings, and among these I wish to mention Cherubino Gambardella, Beniamino Servino, Gabriele Mastrigli, Marco Brizzi, Fabrizia Ippolito, Alessandro Scandurra, Paolo Pasquini, Elena Manzo, Enrico Cerasi, Stefano Guidarini, Piero Maranghi.

An important opportunity for active contact with the work of Fuksas also comes from my courses at the Faculty of Architecture of Naples Luigi Vanvitelli and the public conference of March 2005, planned and promoted with the usual energy and generosity in Naples by the "Luigi Vanvitelli" Faculty of Architecture and by the dean Alfonso Gambardella.

Profound thanks are also due to my publisher, Skira, and their president Massimo Vitta Zelman, who have never denied me their support and trust.

Finally I wish to dedicate this work to Marta, the indispensable presence to enable me to keep on seeking and writing with passion and serenity.

1970-1990

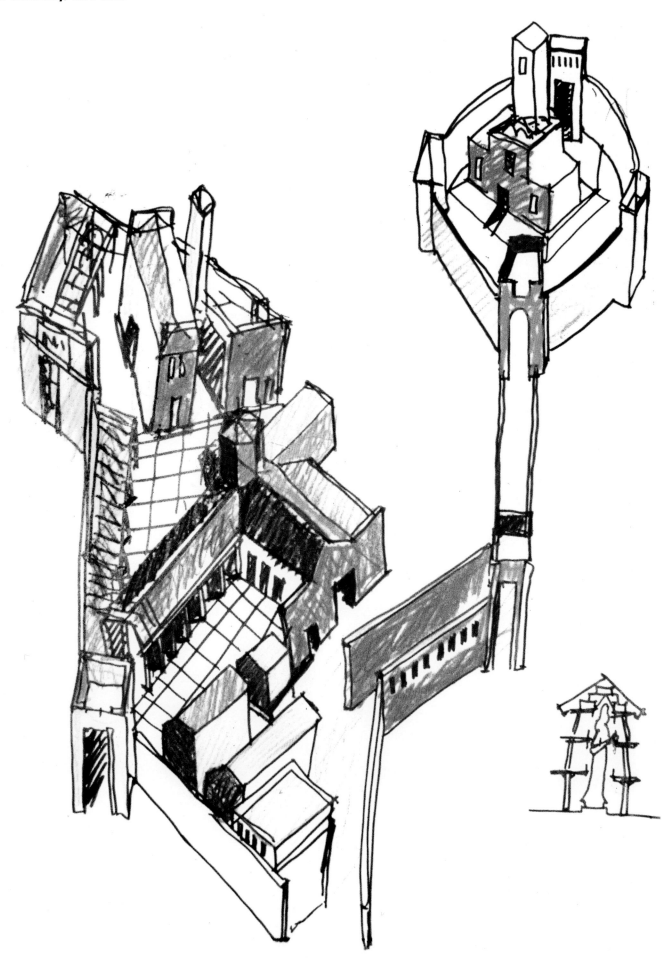

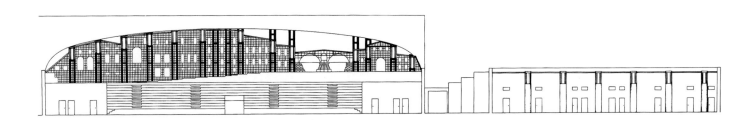

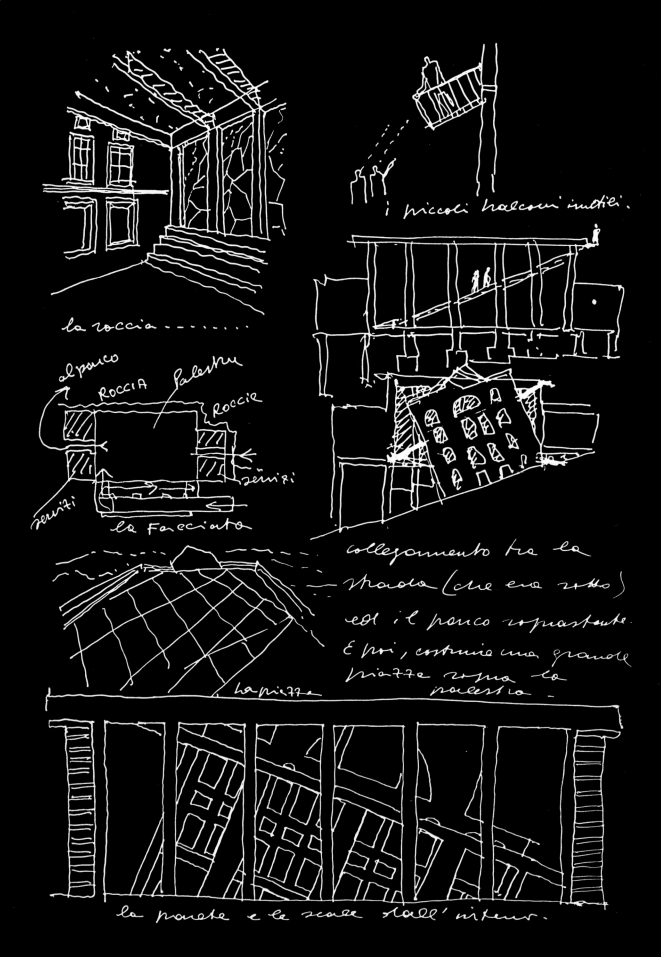

Civita Castellana, Cemetery, 1985-1992

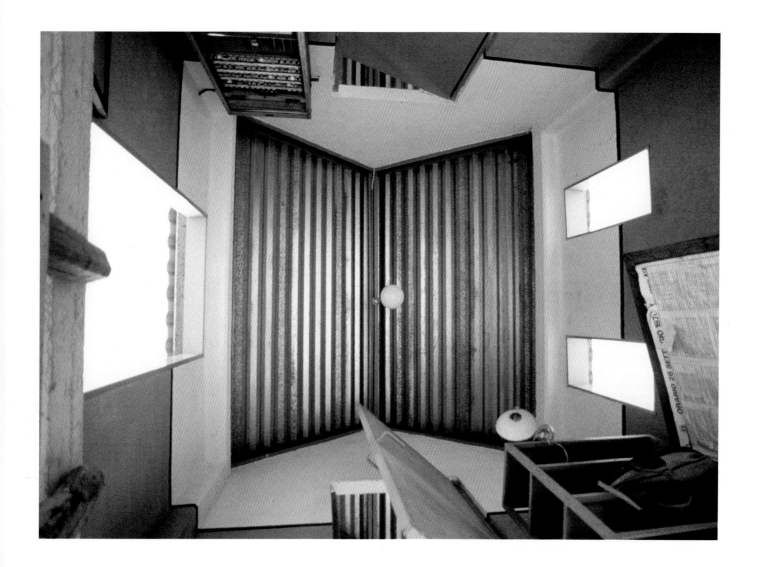

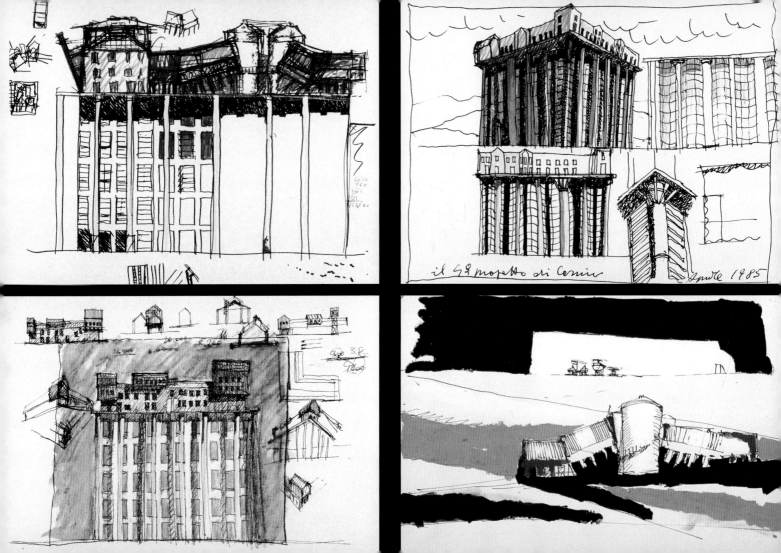

il So moretto di Cormin   Aprile 1985

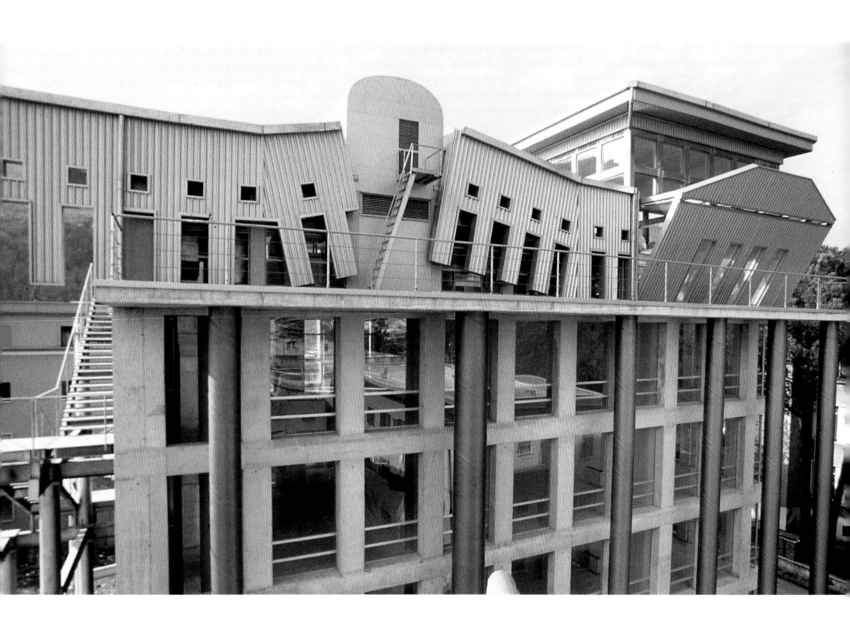

Orvieto, Cemetery (extension), 1984-1991

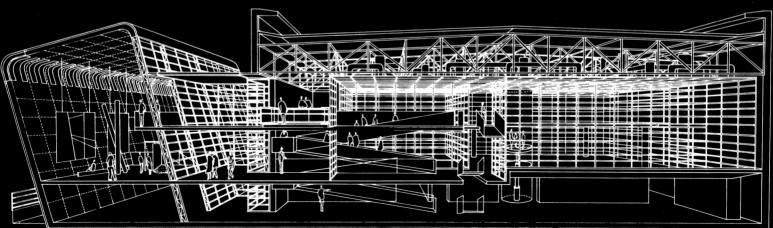

Hamburg, Rebuilding of Vecchio porto district, 1989-1992

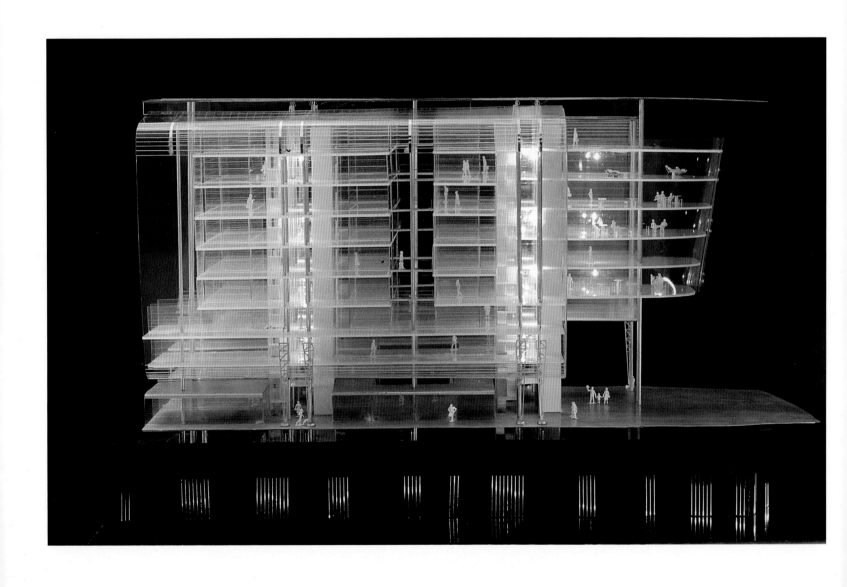

Niaux, Museum of Graffiti, 1988-1993

Noisy-le-Grand, Saint-Exupéry college, 1989-1993

Limoges, Law and Economic sciences Faculty, 1989-1996

Monument, Form, Landscape, Vision:
Massimiliano Fuksas 1970-2005

A cloud traced to brush mutably the regular limits of a transparent box; a glass tongue more than a kilometre long, the new gallery of the future metropolitan city; an opaque container, dark on the outside and alive with cuts bringing the natural light inside; two tall, sharp towers that graze the eastern sky; a strong sign, copper slithering downward to signal an archaic, precious place; a tower-manifesto composed of the joint work of four friends and colleagues; a gymnasium the façade of which suddenly slides, coming to a standstill in the ground; a mystery garden in which to lose yourself to find hidden metaphors.

Massimiliano Fuksas is a problem for those who decide to approach his thirty years of work while avoiding the easy temptation of dismissing it as the sum of an artist's whims and experiments. First of all, because the various linguistic phases expressed (a natural habit for the career path of every true designer who comes to grips with life and the stresses that reality can offer) not only contrast and intersect concretely with the asphyxiated Italian panorama of the seventies and eighties, but also register together some of the most interesting and influential European impulses and research ventures on the contemporary scene.

I believe it would be mistaken to filter Fuksas' experience through the single lens of the Italian telescope; his path appears much more complex and can be assimilated to the parallel histories of other protagonists belonging to his generation, in which the comparison between national identity and heterodox international and multicultural paths began to carry more weight.

Massimiliano Fuksas (1944), Jean Nouvel (1945), Rem Koolhaas (1944), Hans Koolhoff (1945), Otto Stiedle (1943), Will Alsop (1947), Bernard Tschumi (1944) and Toyo Ito (1941): a generation of protagonists of contemporary architecture that was decisive starting from the nineties but above all with paths that, in their difference, have tended to resemble each other in terms of their cultural and research growth curves.

Born during the war, with a late modernist formation without the problem of direct comparison with the Masters, as was the case for the Team X generation, with student life during the sixties with direct or indirect apprenticeships in contact with the Radical experience (from Claude Parent for Nouvel to Kikutake for Ito, passing through Archigram and AA for Fuksas, Tschumi and Koolhaas), with the vital experience of the economic boom, Pop culture and the cultural short circuits that interrelated new instruments and forms of representation of the world of art (Land Art, Conceptual, Informal, Kinetic), comic strips (the arrival of Marvel Comics), advertising, rock music and the first mass concerts, politics, they arrived at their first autonomous professional activities in the early seventies.

It is the story of a generation that is still to be fully investigated and written about, but that in the paths followed and in the works realised affirms important points of convergence that have never intended to be transformed into a "School" or a "Style", but rather have profoundly influenced the contemporary scene from the conceptual and programmatic standpoint through the definition of new key words with which to interpret reality (from *SMLXL*, passing through *Event City*, *Mutations* and *Less Aesthetics/More Ethics*) and a design approach strongly conditioned by both a conceptual and a popular vision of the object of architecture.

In all the various cases, furthermore, a precarious equilibrium continues to exist between national identity – evident in the training paths, in the early works but still strongly traceable in the design matrices expressed by the authors – and tension towards the exterior, towards an international dimension that has definitively confirmed their fame and influence.

This was a condition that had a slow evolution during the whole of the 20th century, from the untiring capacity for international aggression of Le Corbusier, the first true global architect of the century, to the transnational networks of the CIAM and Team X, but only met with a definitive maturation on the individual scale with this generation, who, through their worldwide success, confirmed that dangerous interweaving of media, marketing, circulation of ideas and information flow that currently marks the international scene.

Another important element for the definition of a general frame of reference concerns the relationship with the contemporary city. This generation has had to come to grips with a worldwide urban situation that is profoundly changed and unstable.

Their lives and experiences registered the metropolitan building boom at first hand (in Italy, for example, the major cities increased their surface areas an average of five times over) and they began to operate directly in the new territories of the world's metropolises with a profoundly different attitude from the modernist moralism that saw every periphery as an evil to be eradicated.

These designers' attitude, on the other hand, was realistic but not nihilistic, pragmatic and visionary at the same time, experimental to the extent to which architecture must provide new answers to new questions that arise from a changeable metropolitan situation, complex and densely stratified. So the Mediatheque in Rezé by Fuksas (1987-91), the Tower of Wind in Yokohama by Ito (1986), the Nemausus I houses in Nîmes by Nouvel (1985-1987), the Park of La Villette in Paris by Tschumi (1982-1997), the Kunsthal in Rotterdam by Oma-Rem Koolhaas (1987-1992), in their profound diversity, all express a new and different attitude towards the contemporary city, representing a violent break with the Postmodern drift, but above all a design gaze combining conceptual reflection on the body of architecture, the otherness of the object with respect to the surrounding context through unexpected spatiality and materiality and the search for a different experience and the wonder of contemporary architecture.

These works do not condemn the surrounding context, rather they welcome it and rework it, transforming it into a precious resource; together they are viruses introduced into the system to change it profoundly and attempts at a research into the form of architecture that does not come about as compositional action[1] but rather as conceptual and plastic reaction to the phenomena of reality[2].

When in 1986, at the invitation of François Geindre, Mayor of Hérouville-Saint-Clair, Fuksas called upon his three friends and colleagues, Stiedle, Alsop and Nouvel, to compose a tower designed in fragments individually and separately (the four authors sent the projects via fax, which were assembled together), the author not only performed an unprecedented action but also marked the mature advance of a new generation of designers. The definitive project is surprising on account of its brutality and force; the autonomy of the different contributions is never placed in question, but controls the conceptual dimension of the operation; by designing the base of the tower and endowing it with hefty railway carriages[3] indicating the desire to transform the tower into a nomadic object, Fuksas pays homage to the cult of metropolitan mobility of Radical culture, from the Archigram Walking City to Cedric Price's Fun Palace and the Walking Truck by Friedrich St. Florian.

1987 was a decisive year of change for Fuksas, a vital and necessary pivotal point for the evolution of his work and fortunes. It was the year of the first important French commissions for Paris Ilot Rue Candie-Passage Saint Bernard, for the Mediatheque in Rezé, the Maison de la Confluence in Avoine, as well as the invitation to the competition for the port of Hamburg[4].

Tour Européenne, Hérouville-Saint-Clair, with William Alsop, Jean Nouvel and Otto Stiedle, 1986, model

As recently as 1986, his project for the competition by invitation for the Promenade Plantée Bastille in Paris had shocked some with the provocative brutality of a new urban machine capable of assembling and assimilating into itself fragments of cities, gardens and infrastructures[5]. It was a collage born ideally as the synthesis of the planning processes and the works built by Fuksas up to that moment in the countryside of the Roman province starting from 1970.

Massimiliano Fuksas' success lies precisely in the recognition of these "diverse", wild[6] and irrepressible works by the French. Patrice Goulet, the true "discoverer" of Fuksas' work[7] and one of his most acute critics, launched him through "Architecture d'Aujourd'hui" between 1982 and 1985 with a series of significant articles and interviews[8] in contrast with the silence and apparent indifference the Italian critics had reserved for him during the whole of the previous decade[9]. The French discovery earned him an invitation to the Biennial of Architecture in Paris in 1984. Together with the criticism, unexpected effects were produced by two trips organised by the IFA to Rome for local administrators to visit contemporary architecture (a practice worth copying by our poor clients in public administration!) with the meeting between Jacques Floch, the young socialist mayor of Rezé and the works in Anagni and Paliano, which led to an invitation for Fuksas to visit the French town and work with the municipal authority.

We should reflect on the reasons for Massimiliano Fuksas' French success, but I believe that at the basis of this success lay a cultural process that anticipated the Italian contemporary dynamics by at least a decade: the active use that politics has always made of architecture as a communicative "medium", a gatherer of consensus and an element with a strong civil presence, together with the awareness that only contemporary architecture is the bearer of strong, innovative identities to be introduced like viruses into the apparently uniform fabric of postwar new towns. And Fuksas' work of the seventies, almost all of public origin, presented itself, with its figuratively subversive charge and each time with strong spatial identities, as one of the recipes that were potentially interesting in the eyes of the new French politics.

Likewise, it is essential to consider the centrality of Fuksas' French experience from our own (Italian, that is) point of view not only for the fundamental evolution of his linguistic experience but above all for the reality check that the Roman author was forced to conduct from 1987 to the late nineties with an impressive acceleration of opportunities, of orders and works, almost all in France, which enabled Fuksas to experiment with the force and also the limits of his design action and also to verify this almost in real time, in the field, on the worksite.

These opportunities were generated by the great French period of architecture competitions on a local and national scale, which ensured that Fuksas participated in six competitions in 1988, 16 in 1989, 18 in 1990 and 10 in 1991, winning no less than 11 of them[10].

In architecture, when talent cannot combine with the capacity to give life and shape to its own intuitions, there is a risk of only creating nightmares (those of reason) and giving life to all too many celibate machines. This is what happened, and to a lesser degree has unfortunately continued to happen in Italy for at least twenty years now.

In France Fuksas became a European, an international architect, but above all he found a suitable clientele, used to relating to contemporary architecture and with the possibility of wanting new works for a society in profound transformation.

Yet let us not forget that the first, difficult experiments took place in the Italian provinces, one of the still vital resources of our national identity on account of their polycentric, stratified and complex

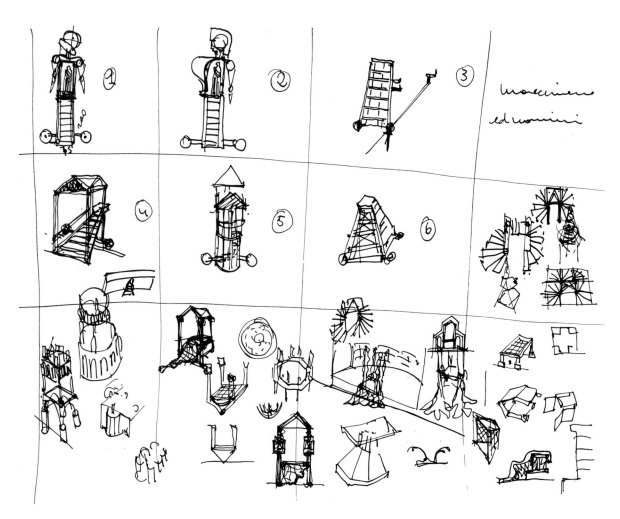

"Machines and Men", reflection starting out from de Chirico, 1976

character, in which a strong sense of tradition, the land and the location can coexist with unprecedented aspirations to contemporaneity and experimentation. In Italy Fuksas' success gained in the major urban centres took place very slowly and only after his significant experience beyond the Alps (Rome, project for Stazione Termini, 1997, Turin Porta Palazzo, 1998, Rome EUR 1999, Rome ASI 2000, and so on) while it was thanks to the meeting with the mayors of small Italian towns, entrepreneurs and artisans still aware of their own art, that Fuksas was able to try out new things and to experiment, precisely beginning from the gymnasium in Sasso Corvaro, built in 1973, a few dozen metres from a fortress by Francesco di Giorgio Martini.

I like to think of Fuksas' thirty-year career path as a slow, inexorable metamorphosis in which the languages inevitably change with time, but in which personal obsessions remain and are sharpened, their profound nature remaining strong. I believe that architectural language is a tool rather than a goal for Fuksas, an aware instrument, but subject to the phases brought about by the meeting with other experiences, by a complex internal maturation, by the context with which he comes to grips, and which he encounters with curious physicality, by the very transversal stimuli that he continually seeks. While at the same time it is possible to link projects and works that are also very far removed from each other in time through less conventional elements, more tied to a sensory condition of the space, to its experience and discovery, to its relationship with light and the seasons, to the active mediation that he seeks with the surrounding landscape. From a certain standpoint, Massimiliano Fuksas is a very traditional architect, and his experience of living in Rome in his youth has played a very important part in this.

His way of filtering his initial reflection on the project through painting, with a technique that has slowly evolved from oil to the more immediate acrylic on plastic canvas[11], but that conserves a decisive and necessary founding value for the author in the gesturality of the action, is traditional, almost ancient.

And his traditional approach also lies in conceiving architecture each time as a monumental pres-

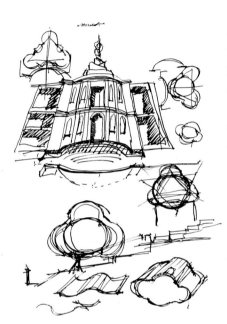

Study sketch and reflection on Borromini's San Carlino, 1974

ence in the context in which it is positioned, where by monument we understand what Ernesto Rogers defined as *"an expression that originally derives from the concepts of 'memory' and 'warning', from the Latin 'moneo' and 'memini'. The original meaning of the concept expressed the psychological activity of memory; from it, we arrive through a process at the meaning of 'prevalently artistic fact that must be remembered and therefore serve as a warning to future generations. [...] But other meanings can be discovered in the semantic and morphological origin of the word 'monument', and it is probably the concept of 'monstrum', that is, of a natural or artistic fact that, due to its exceptionality, is worthy of attention: to show oneself and therefore to be looked at. [...] The wider, the more alive, the richer, the more throbbing, more human our horizon becomes"*[12].

This dimension looks in parallel at two conditions that are necessary and complementary, even if on different scales, the former of the work of architecture as a dynamic fragment of city and landscape, the latter as a location of people's emotional and sensory experiences.

In both cases the definition of the scene is unstable; it does not look at architecture as a "fixed scene"[13] but feverishly records the surrounding reality and the author's insights.

If there is a strong evolution, it is rather in the methods with which Fuksas has related architecture with the idea of city over the years, though remaining against the background of the cultural sediment of the Italian scene of the sixties and seventies, which saw architecture as a natural place of reflection on the city and its nature, rather than an isolated fragment. Such reflections, begun with the decisive theoretical and project work contributions of Giancarlo De Carlo, Vittorio Samonà and Ludovico Quaroni, came to a phase of maturity with Aldo Rossi, Vittorio Gregotti, Franco Purini and therefore with

Lotus magazine, edited by Pierluigi Nicolin, defining an important identity for Italian architecture in relation to the international debate.

But the unusual – compared to his other experiences – path embarked upon by Fuksas in the seventies seemed to aim at other objectives, with different cultural and figurative instruments, which undoubtedly were to cost him the distrust of a significant section of the academic world and the Italian critics. The Roman architect's cultural horizon appeared to be different from the context[14] in which it was formed; if it started from the presence of Zevi, Quaroni and Portoghesi and from comparison with them, in reality it has lived from a strong personal experience in relation to painting, poetry and student activism. His intense personal relationships with Giorgio Caproni and Pier Paolo Pasolini, with the writings of Galvano della Volpe, with art historian Giorgio Castelfranco – who played a key part in his figurative formation and who was to introduce him to De Chirico – his family history, with the Lithuanian origins of his father and his early childhood spent in Austria with his maternal grandmother and also the vibrant Rome of the sixties, with the occupation, the clashes at Valle Giulia, the intense artistic life, the avant-garde galleries and the arrival of Pop and North American conceptual art, have all made Fuksas an anomalous figure with respect to the Roman scene.

The need to *make a city* by building new architecture passed into his first works through a strongly literary and also figurative approach[15].

The city and its idea have been introjected into his work through the reworking of certain rhetorical figures that were very much used by the Italian architectural design culture of those years, the maze, the theatre, the observatory[16], and in the design sketches for the buildings in Paliano, Anagni, Civita Castellana he worked obsessively on the assembly and dismantling of classical and baroque architectural fragments, fragments copied over the years and re-examined as

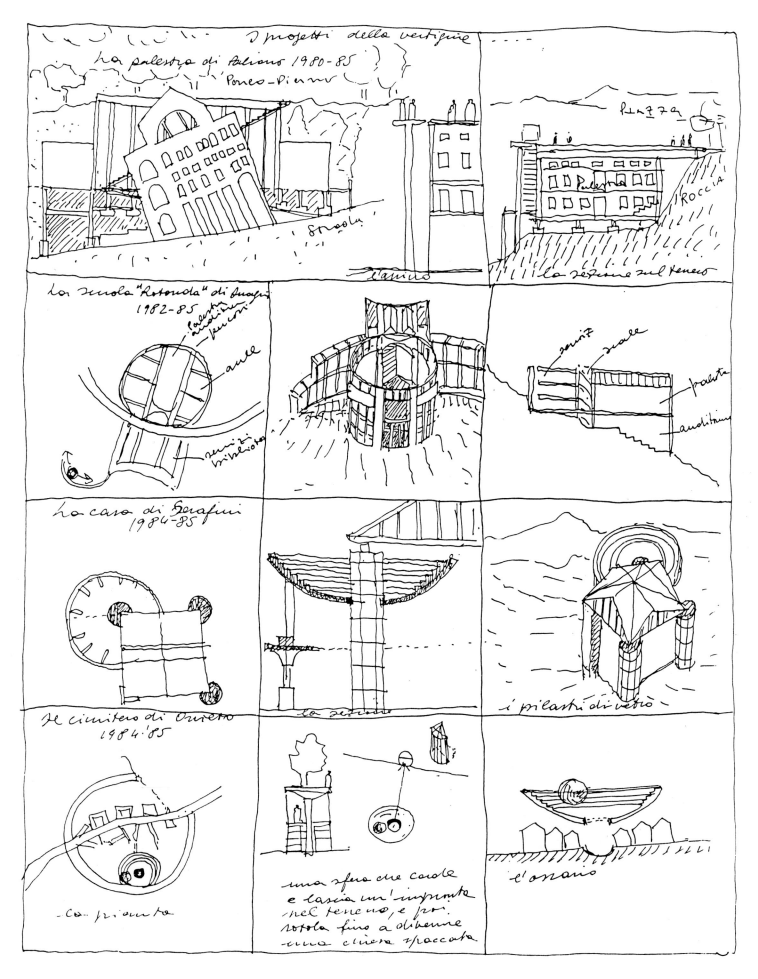

I progetti della vertigine

La palestra di Paliano 1980-85
Porcos-Piumo

Piazza

Palestra

Roccia

la sezione sul terreno

strada

La scuola "Rotonda" di Anagni
1982-85
palestra
auditorium
percorsi
aule

servizi
biblioteca

zenit
sale

palestra

auditorium

La casa di Serafini
1984-85

la sezione

i pilastri di vetro

Il cimitero di Orvieto
1984-'85

una sfera che rotola
e lascia un'impronta
nel terreno, e poi
rotola fino a diventare
una chiesa spaccata

l'ossario

la pianta

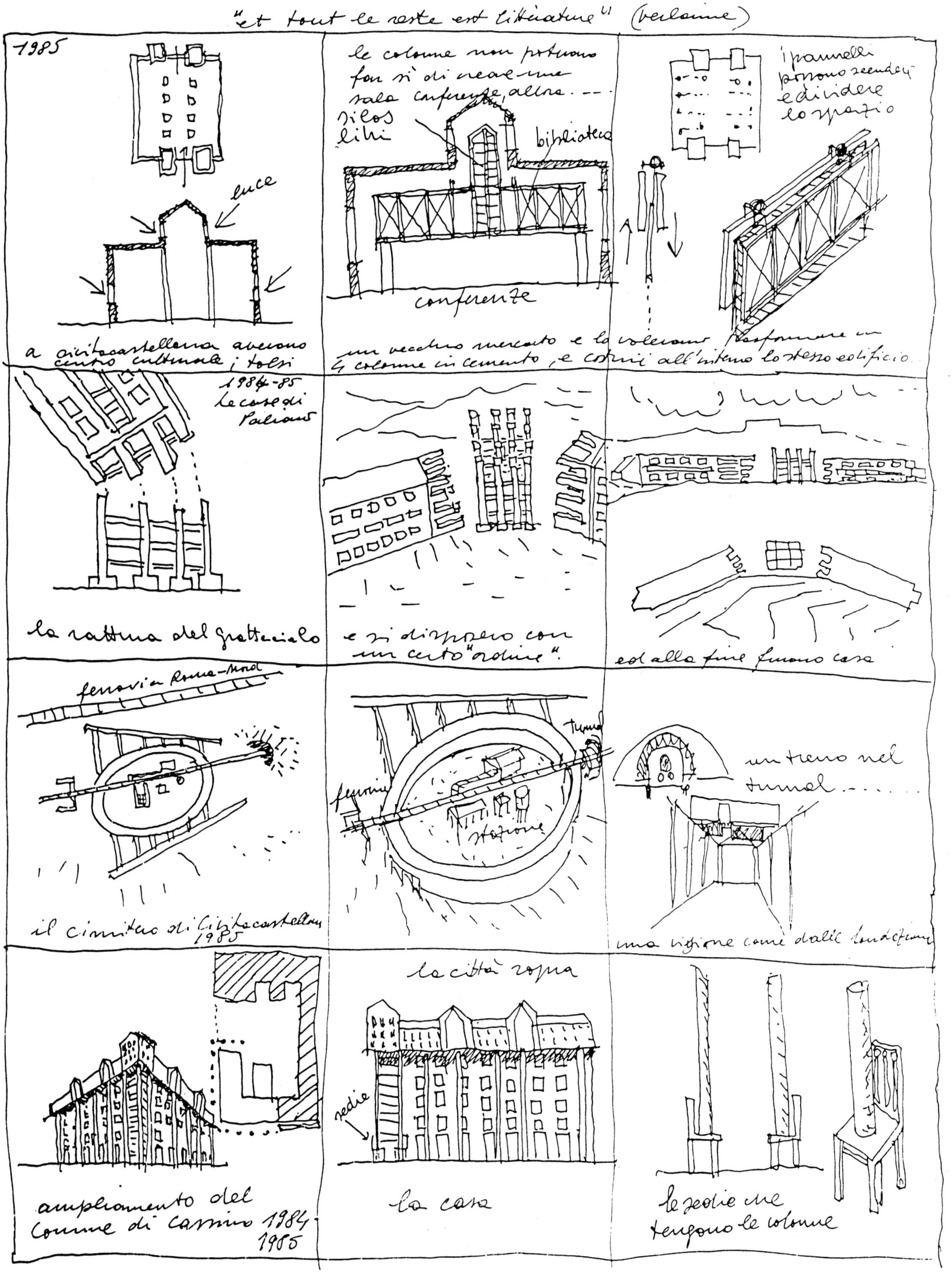

"et tout le reste est littérature" (verlaine)

1985

luce

a civitacastellana avevano
centro culturale; tolsi

le colonne non potevano
far sì di creare una
sala conferenze, allora...
silos libri

biblioteca

conferenze

i pannelli
possono scendere
e dividere
lo spazio

un vecchio mercato e lo volevano trasformare in
4 colonne in cemento, e costruì all'interno lo stesso edificio...

1984-85
le case di
Paliano

la rottura del grattacielo

e si disposero con
un certo "ordine".

ed alla fine furono case

ferrovia Roma-Nord

il cimitero di Civitacastellana
1985

tunnel

ferrovia

stazione

un treno nel
tunnel......

una visione come dalle diligenze

ampliamento del
Comune di Cassino 1984-
1985

la città sogna

sedie

la casa

le sedie che
tengono le colonne

51

through they constituted an unlikely abacus of elements and materials for the project. But the game – because it is a game – did not stop at assembly but sought new paths, attempting to abolish ideologically the separation between plan, front view and section, reversing the points of view so as to find an unlikely philosopher's stone of architecture capable of resolving contradictions long latent in the body of architecture, overturning the accepted conventions. And likewise the project for the competition for the Business District in Florence (1976) was transformed into a first attempt to take shape in the Sports Hall in Anagni (1979-1986), where the design of the plan became the façade of the building, an anamorphosis of design practice that transformed the glass walls into a screen capable of projecting *urban shadows* inside the gymnasium.

And the literary, narrative dimension became more brutally sophisticated, to show architecture as a complex mechanism and at the same time the product of a sought-after gesturality. The bent façade of the gymnasium in Paliano (1979-1985) was undoubtedly the highest and strongest moment of this approach, because it became a manifesto and a landscape together (a break with the sequence of anonymous villas that anticipate the building but also a sense of the quake that occurred in the territory) but it is also experience of the space, becoming an external ramp and also an unlikely grid with which to read the landscape from inside the building. A decidedly more radical gesture compared to the more refined (in linguistic and construction terms) Town Hall in Cassino (1980-1990), in which the top of the new public building is shaken to describe an urban landscape that can no longer lives from harmony and definite rules.

This way of making and narrating the city in the encounter with the French experience has progressively been purified of the whole metaphorical and literary charge and has simply becomes a narration, construc-

tion of routes and spaces introjected into the body of the architecture, allowing the idea of a complex experience of the body of architecture, conceived as a vital fragment of the city, to appear on the façades.

Cassino and the competition for the Promenade Planteé Bastille in Paris (1986) were the moment of change and the ambitious restructuring of the Rue Candie-Passage Saint Bernarde block, again in Paris (1987-1992), the materialisation of this change, which in the long project process led to the construction of a fragment of city built on the sequence of spaces and diversified functions. A small urban megastructure, 130 metres in length, in which the wave of aluminium covering the roof of the first building becomes the narrative and visual line of the new landscape.

The dimensions of the maze, the theatre and the observatory disappear only as rhetorical figures and remain to animate conceptually the conceiving of many of the French projects.

A thin line in fact links the urban maze of the school of Civita Castellana (1982-1986) or the theatrical staging of the cemetery for the same town (1985-1992) with the fragmented and metropolitan introversion of the training and research unit in Tours (1991), with the school citadel of the Maximilien Perret High School in Alfortville (1995-1997) or with the smaller, more sophisticated introjection of the Ferrari Centre in Maranello (1999-2005) and the Frankfurter Ziel Projekt in Frankfurt (2002-2007).

Over the years the urban tension of Fuksas' works has shifted slowly and has seemed to focus on the further change occurring in the last decades of the century from the concept of diffused city to that of megalopolis and therefore from architecture as urban fragment to that of architecture as megastructure and fragment of territory[17]. It was first and foremost a widespread cultural evolution that Fuksas consecrated with the Venice Biennial directed by him in 2000, but also a slowly emerging awareness as a result of the

Paliano School Building, plan of the ground floor

Civita Castellana Cemetery, plan of the ground floor

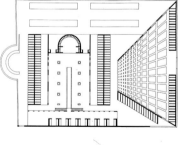

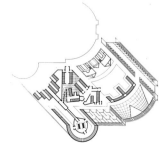

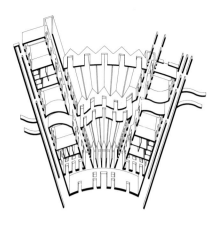

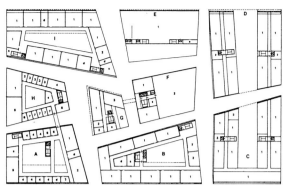

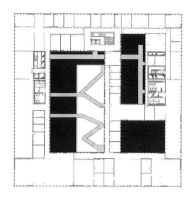

Civita Castellana School Building,
plan of the ground floor

Tours, Training and Research Center,
plan of the second level

Maranello, Ferrari Operational Headquarters,
plan of the second level

project work experiences that he gained from the early nineties, in which the physical and programmatic dimension increased in scale and complexity and in which the scenarios themselves changed, moving the author from the French scene to the global one.

The design of the roof, of the completion of the buildings that Fuksas designed, seemed to be the first thing to register this jump of sensitivity and scale.

The tops of architectures have always been very much exploited by Fuksas from the functional viewpoint, both as large covered roof terraces overlooking the surrounding landscape (could it have been the daily experience of the large terraces of Roman homes?) and as rhetorical elements to produce a sense of wonder in the visitor; we need only think of the gymnasium in Paliano, the long roof sequence of playing fields for Rue Candie-Passage Saint Bernarde or the terraces of the Perret High School.

But as soon as the Roman architect covered the large complex with a soft metal grid, as in the competition for a large shopping centre in Hérouville-Saint Clair (1989), we suddenly witnessed an important jump of scale that transformed a large architecture into a fragment of metropolitan landscape.

It was a decisive gesture that anticipated a long series of experiments into the relationship between roof, territorial sign and architecture on s large scale that were to lead first to the commercial complex in Salzburg (1994-1997) with its red metal wave as a cover for the car park and then, through a series of other competitions that from the Adidas *World of Sport* in Hezogenaurach (1999), the Salzburg stadium (1999), the Freizeit-und-Einkaufszentrum in Berne (2000) tended towards the progressive dematerialisation of the roof, we arrive directly at the recently completed project for the new Milan Fair (2003-2005), in which this long development that sees a large work of architecture become both a territorial infrastructure and a fragment of landscape seems to be completed.

Observing some of the projects designed and completed between the late nineties and 2005 with a different gaze, we can register the changes and metamorphoses of many of the attitudes and obsessions that are recurrent in the works of Massimiliano Fuksas, which are not exhausted with the general approach, constituting the work, but above all define the designer's gaze.

Despite the enlarging of dimensions and administrative complexity of the more recent works, Fuksas' project methodology seems to follow a path that has nevertheless remained unchanged over time, passing from very private pictorial design to intense experimentation in the workshop with the construction of models on various scales, only arriving at the end at the design proper. Furthermore, the author's attention seems above all to dwell only on certain pivotal spatial points or on a few meditated details to enable the overall architectural space to be controlled through a synthetic and intuitive interpretation of the construction and its experience over time.

In all the projects, we never witness the affirmation of a stylistic trademark, but rather the continuous reflection on the identification of tensions conceived thinking about the constructed space and above all the emotional and sensory impact the visitor can feel.

The seductive temptation is always very strong in the reflection that Fuksas brings to architecture and combines well with the strongly narrative will inherent in every building designed by him.

Fuksas loves to work on the spaces between things, on tensions that can be made visible, on separations and slight gaps that immediately produce contradictory and complementary sensations.

It could be said that Fuksas reasons in a Venturian fashion, in the sense of not recognising the modernist exclusion of "either/or", but rather working on the contemporary force of "both/and", on its vitality, on the force of contradictions.

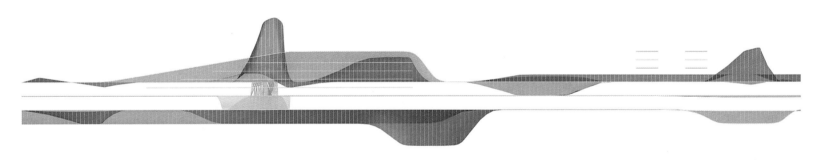

Castorama Supermarket, Hérouville-Saint-Clair, 1989, competition

Europark 1, Salzburg, 1994-97, detail of the roofing of the elevated car parks

Freizeit-und-Einkaufszentrum, Bern, 1999, competition, detail of the longitudinal section

New Milan Trade Fair Centre, 2002-05, detail of the roofing of the pavilions of the central gallery and the Forum

But as a Venturian character, Fuksas remains a modern and universal architect, in whose work the awareness of the construction of space passes through the almost cinematographic construction of locations, of their discovery, of the emotions and pauses they are capable of generating, of the intentional dialogue with the surrounding landscape and the natural light, of colour as material for architectural action and also of the horizon of the culture of the Modern as a natural sphere in which to move.

And so the aware construction of tensions passes through staircase structures, always metal, always coloured, often at the centre of the scene, as in the case of the Hanse-Forum in Hamburg (1998-2002), at the Perret High School in Alfortville, in the bowels of the Twin Towers in Vienna (1995-2000) or in the open patio of the Ferrari Centre.

But the tensions are also moulded by the light touching of large masses or of contradictory elements, such as the beams cut off in the air of the residences in Paliano (1983-1987), the black box of the Mediatheque in Rezé, which is tilted away from the existing building, or the horizontal and vertical cut with which he marks the Maison des Artes in Bordeaux (1992-1995), a dress rehearsal for the fascinating rising of the upper floors of the Ferrari Centre, passing through the first caged and then uncovered bubbles of the Faculty of Law in Limoges (1993-1996) and the suspension bridge of the Twin Tower in Vienna, which indicates the great proximity of the two blades of glass and black steel.

Contrasts constructed by moulding light and materials together, as is shown in the project for the synagogue in Dresden (1997), in the Peace Centre in Jaffa (1998-2007) and in the centre at Porta Palazzo in Turin (1998-2006) and finally in the church in Foligno (2001-2006), a series of buildings designed and built on the same principle that sees a construction closed to the outside, striated by horizontal graftings of structural glass on the outside walls and by unexpected cuts of light that mould the internal section of the main construction.

Tension also means respectful comparison and not strong opposition, revealing a dimension of Fuksas that is attentive to the pre-existing physical space in which he intervenes, which is resolved with strong control of the materials used and its spatial rendering. The first work built, the gymnasium in Sasso Corvaro, shows an elegant dialogue with the nearby fortress of Francesco di Giorgio, then in the Parco della Fontana del Diavolo in Paliano (1977-1978) it becomes almost imitation with the natural element but also with the idea of a new sixteenth-century garden of *mystery and marvel*. Then the INEAA in Rouen (1990-1992), in which the new metal roof becomes a perfect completion of the solid old construction, arriving at the projects for the Gallery in the Aldobrandini stables in Frascati (1995) or for the new Roman studio, in which the attention to the dialogue with the pre-existing building becomes light, almost withdrawing but without any sense of inferiority, as in the recent case for the enlargement of the Mall in Eindhoven, where Fuksas sets himself in relation to the building by Giò Ponti with the respect that is due to the work of a great Master, creating openings that look out at the coloured ceramics of the external coverings of the old building.

Yet tensions are often built on the clash/confrontation between a regular, rational element and an exceptional happening, as though to make visible the necessary joint presence of the universal rule of "both/and".

This applies for the almost strident dialogue between the pavilions and the gallery of the Milan Fair, in which the interplay of reflections (water on the ground, the mirroring and opaque steel walls, the orange surfaces) is multiplied by the vaulted cells and the various apertures in the buildings, such as for the new Congress Centre in Rome, in

which Fuksas visualises the idea of a cloud caged in a regular transparent container, but which we also find in the bubbles covered in copper that puncture the external glass surface of the Faculty of Law in Limoges (1989-1996) or in the unhinged façade of the gymnasium in Anagni.

There is another interesting parallel between two stories, two destinies that are marking Italian and international architecture; namely the closeness/distance between Fuksas and Renzo Piano.

Friends[18], both welcomed and launched in France, equally snubbed for a long time by the Italian academic scene, proud of their own autonomy and their italianness, among the few architects known to the media, both attracted to and interested in a reflection that is first of all in project work terms from the relationship with megastructures or in general with the monumental and urban dimension of architecture.

Reflection that becomes experimental research applied directly to the project and filtered by a use of technology and construction technique that marks the watershed between the two authors, becoming in the former case a signature and in the latter case an instrument to affirm a plastic and sensory dimension of the body of architecture.

Even when, at the end of the nineties, Fuksas seemed to embrace a massive use of digital technology to design and represent his new works[19], we can easily see that the use is solely instrumental to moving the limit of control onto the conception and realisation of forms that were inconceivable until a few years ago, unless at unsustainable costs.

We need only compare the rather rough and brutal line of the spherical classrooms covered in zinc for the Faculty of Law in Limoges (1989-1996) with the elegant and sophisticated design of the crystal and steel *bubbles* for the Nardini Centre (2002-2004) in Bassano del Grappa to realise the leap forward made and also the countless possibilities that can be unveiled to a designer who makes research into form the focus of his work.

Technological invention is a necessity to give form to a vision or to an image obstinately pursued. When, in designing the roof of the raised car park at Europark 1 in Salzburg, Fuksas evoked the memory of the ride on huge waves in the film *Point Break* by Kathryn Bigelow, or in dealing with the one and a half kilometre long glass gallery for the new Fair in Milan, he decided to simulate a natural landscape; the creative mechanism moves from one image to a series of possible technological solutions that not only allow it but also silently strengthen its perception.

The low/high tech application and the different, often sophisticated technical solutions, become invisible elements, not flaunted, but below the skin, reinforcing the overall perception of the space, its environmental quality. These are elements that combine with the definition that Fuksas gives today of the concept of megastructure, as of a "benevolent"[20] and necessary monumental element.

On one hand, the exceptional scale as a transcending of the concept of city in favour of that of a complex organism, able to react dynamically to the stimuli that the metropolis continues to produce, but on the other, the concept of "benevolence" expresses a content that I believe to be much more explosive and socially innovative.

That is, the need for architecture to still be the bearer of new visionary forms with a content of unprecedented realism, in which the benevolent attention towards users, the quality of their lives and everyday activity becomes a central element of architectural thought.

"Benevolent" understood as aware attention to individuals, their desires and drives, without falling into the trap of the fundamentalism of the happy utopia for all as a result of this, but with a new form of visionary realism in which architecture takes responsibility for producing new visions for society and works as the product of a form of listening to the deep heart of the metropolis[21].

"Benevolence" also as the expression of project research for the construction of locations of well-being, happy with the physical and environmental quality they manage to produce.

I believe this is one of the great challenges that contemporary architecture must meet in the next few years, a new form of listening rather than a new Empire style, a return to the fragile scale of man and the equally delicate one of the landscape, spaces capable of exciting without crushing, capable of welcoming rather than teaching to live, locations capable of responding to the still unexpressed demands of the complex and heterogeneous societies that architecture will find itself accommodating.

New Trade Fair Centre, Rho-Pero;
the architecture and the new scale
of the landscape: detail of the roofs

[1] "Aprés avoir lutté contre le réalisme en montrant que la réalité était toujours une illusion, il a réintroduit la narration en superposant à chacun de ses projects des histoires, des images et des rêves. Il a défait ensuite le lien qui emprisonnait la form à la function puis s'est attaqué à la dictature du dessin, à l'obsession de la composition et à la tyrannie de la façade.", in P. Goulet, *Massimiliano Fuksas. 60 projects*, IFA Paris, Edizioni Carte Segrete, Rome 1992, p. 19.

[2] Two long interviews from the late eighties clarify the relationship between project, context and concept in Fuksas' work: M. Pisani, *Dialogo con Massimiliano Fuksas*, in M. Pisani, *Fuksas architetto*, Gangemi Editori, Rome 1988, pp. 65-77; P. Goulet, *Massimiliano Fuksas...* cit.

[3] In the same years, for a very different project, the new cemetery of Civita Castellana, Fuksas created a new landscape composed of a *montage* of urban and construction fragments, reminiscent of the lessons of Gordon Matta Clark and also of surrealist culture, in an elliptical enclosure traversed longitudinally by a railway track.

[4] On the various workshops that came to shape the Hamburg competition, a full-blown "society debut" for Fuksas, on its importance and on the meeting with Alsop, Stiedle and Nouvel, see: P. Goulet, *Massimiliano Fuksas...* cit., pp. 33, 40.

[5] M. Pisani, *op. cit.*, pp. 76-77.

[6] "Vous avez dit sauvage?" is the title of the long interview that Patrice Goulet devoted to Fuksas in issue 239 of "Architecture d'aujourd'hui" of June 1985, where "wild" [sauvage] is one of the adjectives that is fitting for the amazement and curiosity that Fuksas' work produced in Goulet's reading and interpretation, due to its irrepressible force and to its difference from the contemporary production in Italy and France of those years. This content was later to be dealt with systematically and expanded in the monograph from 1992.

[7] "Do you want to talk to us about Patrice Goulet? He is a key personality. He is the critic who has followed me most, but above all I admire him for his courage", in M. Pisani, *op. cit.*, p. 76.

[8] P. Goulet, *Six architectures*, issue 222, September 1982, pp. 23-45; *Un amphithéatre habité par Massimiliano Fuksas*, issue 225, February 1983, pp. 36-37; *Concours Opéra de la Bastille*, issue 231; P. Goulet, *La géométrie entre le réalité et le rêve*, issue 232, April 1984, pp. 12-17; *Projects et réalisations*, issue 232, April 1984, pp. 66-69; *Vous avez dit sauvage? interview de Massimiliano Fuksas par Patrice Goulet*, issue 239, June 1985, pp. 10-15; P. Goulet, *Et tout le reste est littérature*, issue 240, September 1985, pp. 80-100.

[9] Before the initial article from 1982 in "Architecture d'Aujourd'hui", only three short articles had appeared on Fuksas' work: *Spazio Arte*, issue 5, May 1975, pp. 6-7; *Parametro*, issue 63, January-February 1978; *Controspazio*, issues 5-6, September-December 1978.

[10] P. Goulet, *Massimiliano Fuksas... cit.*, pp. 41-42.

[11] The interviews by Pisani and Goulet already mentioned emphasise the relationship between Fuksas and painting, but it is especially in the French monograph that the author attempts to consider in depth his bond with painting, the crisis that takes place with traditional instruments and the "rediscovery" of painting that arose from the challenge with Alsop in the first workshop in Hamburg through a more immediate, gestural and material use brought about by the meeting with the use of acrylic and plastic canvases; P. Goulet, *Massimiliano Fuksas...* cit. p. 33.

[12] E. Nathan Rogers, *Esperienza dell'architettura*, Skira, Milan 1996, second edition, pp. 163-164.

[13] A. Rossi, *Architettura della città*, Marsilio Editori, Padua 1966.

[14] On the Roman context and Fuksas' formation, for the sake of completeness and for the various nuances of interpretation, see also: M. Pisani, *op. cit.*; P. Goulet, *Massimiliano Fuksas...* cit., to which must be added a brief but illuminating essay by G. Muratore, *Stile Fuksas*, in "L'Arca", issue 197, November 2004, pp. 36, 37.

[15] In the interview with Pisani, describing the school in Civita Castellana, Fuksas comments: "The school is a piece of the city, but it is also a city itself". M. Pisani, *op. cit.*, p. 67.

[16] P. Goulet, *Massimiliano Fuksas...* cit., p. 24.

[17] We move from the first, central observation that Fuksas made in the dialogue with Pisani: "In your view, where is architecture going? Into the city. Those who have not understood this are completely out of the game." (M. Pisani, *op. cit.*, p. 77), in the writings, interviews and publications that took place during and as a result of the Biennial in Venice directed by him in 2000: M. Fuksas, P. Conti, *Caos Sublime*, Rizzoli, Milan 2001; M. Fuksas, *Frames*, Actar International, Barcelona 2001.

[18] When Fuksas polemically resigned from the management of the Biennial of Architecture in 2001, one of the few architects who intervened publicly in support of his work was Renzo Piano.

[19] Massimiliano Fuksas' volume, *Frames*, published by Actar in 2001 and admirably designed by Ramon Prat, is a perfect synthesis and representation of Fuksas' digital period.

[20] The term "benevolent megastructure" ("megastruttura gentile") derives from a private conversation with Massimiliano Fuksas in May 2005.

[21] The term "gentle" should also be ascribed to his relationship with Robert Venturi and his idea of "gentle manifesto".

Projects 1995-2005

Fuksas Studio, Rome (Italy)

Massimiliano and Doriana Fuksas's studio in Rome is located in a Renaissance building on Piazza del Monte di Pietà, in the vicinity of Campo dei Fiori. The building, like the majority of constructions from that period, has been subjected to numerous alterations and extensions over the years, culminating in its present configuration, which dates from the work done in 1870.

The project of renovation, carried out to adapt it to its new function, has focused on the restoration of the building in general and the functional conversion of a series of rooms located on several levels. The operation was conducted in an atmosphere of uninhibited respect for the existing construction, whose original structures and the materials have been highlighted by cleaning and waxing the 15th-century masonry. The work of reclamation of the building has made it possible to free the basic volume from subsequent additions and bring to light elements encumbered and concealed by earlier interventions: these included the renewal of the vault of the family chapel and, more generally, the *piano nobile*, galleries and internal staircase.

The Fuksas Studio and Fuksas Design occupy an area of 1100 m^2, distributed on four floors linked by two lifts in glass and steel with a natural finish. The landing on the first floor leads to the entrance, divided from the meeting room by a transparent pane of glass mounted on frames of brushed iron. The view of the common room is filtered by pale sheets of cloth, utilized to project images when necessary. The room is situated in a corner and has one side facing onto the square. The inside walls are treated with slaked lime and natural white pigments and roofed with a coffered ceiling painted with white lacquer. The floor, which is the same throughout the area covered by the project, is made of oak planks treated with wax. On the same level are the reception and other workspaces, which house an original collection of models. The model workshop and design sector are on the second floor, while the architect's room is located higher up. The room is furnished with chairs designed by Arne Jacobsen and has 17th-century wooden doors from the island of Timor. It is roofed with white-painted wooden trusses and a large sliding wall made of iron serves as a backdrop and support for Fuksas's own paintings.

1. *Detail of one of the work spaces*

2. *The lift and a detail of the meeting room*

**Former Aldobrandini Stables, now Museo del Tuscolo, Frascati
(Rome, Italy)**

The pavilion known as the "ex Scuderie Aldobrandini", or former Aldobrandini Stables, faces onto one side of the main square in the centre of Frascati. Today the building houses the Museo del Tuscolo, while in the 17th century it was an outbuilding of the nearby Villa Aldobrandini, of which it constituted the stables and coach house.

The present owner of the structure is the municipality, which in 1989 entrusted Massimiliano and Doriana Fuksas with its renovation and extension, with the aim of setting up a multipurpose cultural centre in the old building, housing an archaeological museum equipped with a conference hall and exhibition spaces for temporary events. The Fuksas Studio decided to operate within the limitations of the context, freeing the construction from the additions accumulated over the course of the last thirty years but without eliminating the traces and modifications left by history.

The external façade has retained its consolidated appearance, characterized by wide openings on the first floor and a large doorway from which the interior of the museum can be glimpsed through the glazed gallery, restoring it to the city. The rooms devoted to the permanent archaeological collection are located on the ground floor, separated from the sectors reserved for temporary exhibitions of contemporary art and the 250 m^2 auditorium. A concrete-and-iron floor slab, set at a distance of 150 cm from the outer walls and supported by metal pillars, means that the room does not look as if it has been subdivided but retains the appearance of a continuous, two-storey-high space, unified by an uninterrupted backdrop of Pompeian red relieved only by the gleam of the precious collection of sculptures.

The archaeological finds are displayed on close-set bronze supports of different heights, arranged almost at random in a central space with a width of 2.60 m constructed of tempered and stratified glass. The translucent panes, embedded directly in the ground and illuminated by a series of iridescent pipes, create a play of refractions and transparencies that seems to amplify the impression of the structure's dematerialization.

1. *Ground floor plan*

2. *View of the gallery*

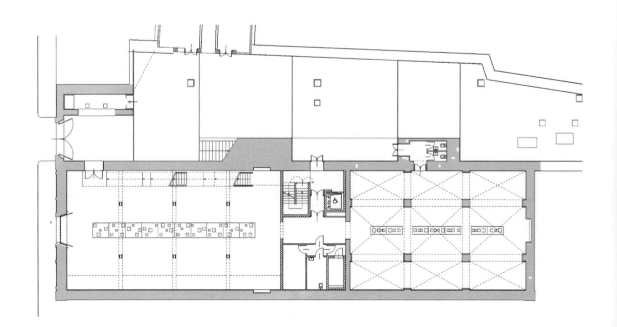

3. *Main elevation*

4. *Longitudinal section G-G*

5. *View of the interior*

6. *Cross section H-H, I-I*

Urban reorganization of the Place des Nations, Geneva (Switzerland)

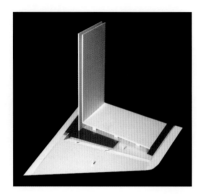

1. *Model, general view*

2. *General layout plan*

The operation entails the urban reorganization of the Place des Nations and an important part of the area in which the international zone is situated. The task was entrusted to Massimiliano Fuksas by the Swiss Department of Public Works and Energy after he had won first prize in the competition held in 1995.

The intervention is restricted to an area for the most part free of existing buildings, in a part of the city where construction is fairly sparse. The buildings that are present consist almost exclusively of the offices of international organizations, arranged at a great distance from each other inside the park,. They are imposing constructions that seek to make a mark on the area with architecture that enhances their image and symbolic and representative weight. Thus green spaces apparently constitute the only means of binding together the various isolated objects that make up the panorama. The urban layout of the Place des Nations, along with the design of the Maison Universelle, new seat of the GATT, the Central Library, a university college and a research institute and the Maison des Droits de l'Homme et des Droits Humanitaires, along with a place of worship for different religious faiths, meet the needs of the reorganization of a disjointed territory.

The proposed system takes the specific characteristics of the place on board and aims at a comprehensive redesign of the landscape, which will define a different distributive and spatial configuration to be put into practice progressively over the long term. The project is committed to working with the existing elements to structure future development in advance, guaranteeing convertibility and flexibility in the utilization of the plots of land and the connections between them.

The enlargement of the road system becomes the pivot of the operation of upgrading and expansion that will make the most of Avenue de la Paix and Avenue de France, the skeleton on which the entire system is based. The two streets, dotted with rows of trees, take on the role of principal axes, ready to accommodate future expansions. In parallel it is planned to realize further secondary infrastructures and footpaths lined with flowers that lead from Route des Morillons to the lake, restoring order and liveability to the setting.

3. *Study sketches*

4. *Model, view from above*

5. *Prospect, general view*

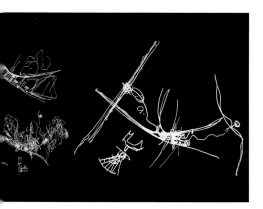
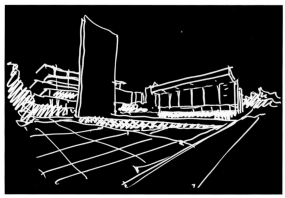
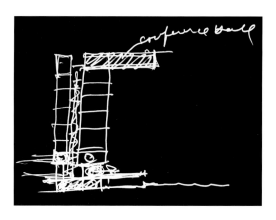

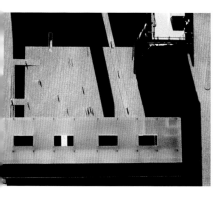

Lycée Maximilien Perret De Vincennes, Alfortville (France)

1-2. *Insertion in the town*

3. *The relationship with the city and the river*

The school is situated along the course of the Seine, at Alfortville, a suburban area to the south-east of Paris that faces onto an industrial district constructed on the opposite bank of the river.

In 1995 the DASES (Direction des Affaires Scolaires) of the Région de l'Île de France commissioned the secondary school, with a library, documentation centre, auditorium and residences for teachers and pupils, from Massimiliano Fuksas. The task was transformed into the realization of a work of architecture conceived as a piece of city capable of recomposing the chaos of the outskirts by giving the context a new geography.

The building is located on an extremely irregular and restrictive site between residential roads and high-rises, but exploits its potentialities to the maximum, gaining light and open spaces through the insertion of a large platform at a height of 7 m above ground level. Under the horizontal slab are set the large windows of a restaurant, the laboratories and the facilities for the teaching of technology, while the classrooms are located on the upper level. The solution adopted creates a division between the two levels, which maintain a dialogue through ample cuts made in the walls to allow light to penetrate into the courtyards and the areas underneath.

The complex, which is oriented towards the south, houses 1600 students, between departments, classrooms and laboratories built out of a variety of materials, including concrete, zinc, glass and brick. Each area is closely connected with the main entrance to the north-east. The entrance hall provides access to the library faced with red zinc, the ovoid auditorium, the headmaster's offices and the more isolated block that will be used as the janitor's house.

The project envisages no symmetry and every choice is aimed at attaining a continuous spatial dynamics measured by the superimposed horizontal layers and animated by a restless succession of bridges, stairs, ramps, roads and paths that open up to the city, extending into the surrounding areas.

4. *The main front onto the street*

5. *Study sketches*

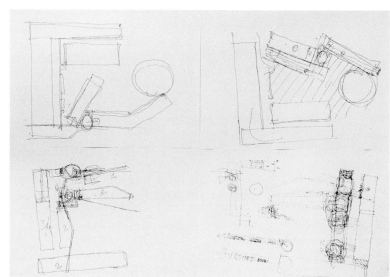

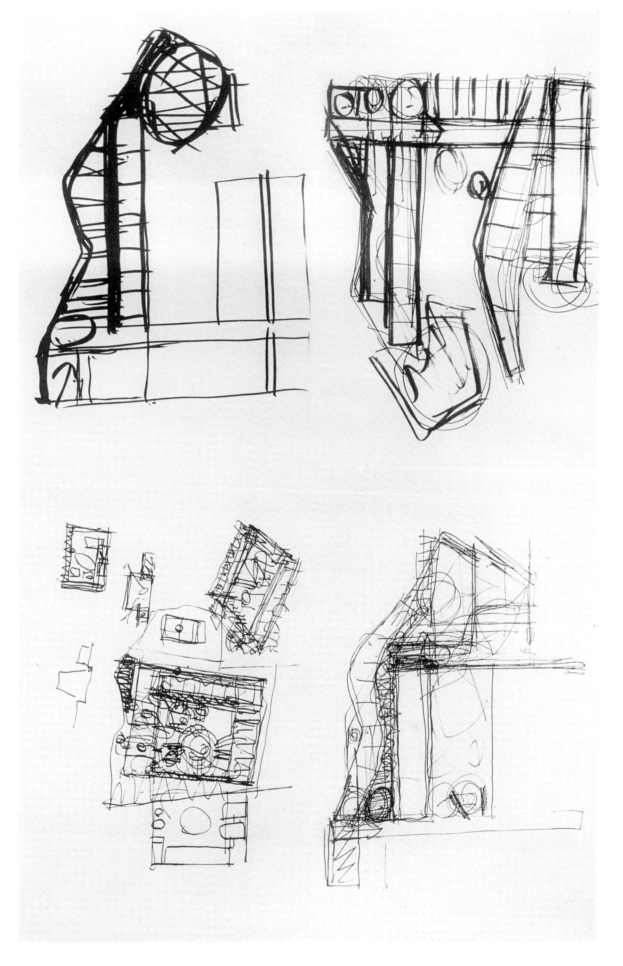

7. *Detail of the roofing and terraces*

8. *The front of the offices and classrooms*

9. *The stratified system of community spaces, classrooms*

12. *Detail of the spaces providing access to the classrooms*

13. *The system of roofs and public bridges as a terrace overlooking the city*

1-3. *Study sketches*

The complex stands on the southern edge of Vienna, in a slightly raised peripheral area, which indicates at a distance the access to the capital from the motorway coming from Trieste, former port of the Austro-Hungarian empire. Since the 19th century the site has housed the Wienerberger quarries and brick kilns, and the company is still the owner of most of the land and the promoter, along with the public administration, of the creation of a new residential and service district. The scheme has been completed with the competition for the Twin Towers and the Wienerberg City Masterplan, won by Massimiliano Fuksas in 1995.

The programme envisaged two office blocks with an annexed entertainment centre, multiscreen cinema, restaurants and underground car park for 1000 vehicles, along with a residential sector equipped with services and infrastructures. Fuksas has conceived a fluid system, capable of holding

a dialogue with the existing structures and establishing a connection, without upheavals, between intensely built-up areas and green spaces. A project regulated by the simultaneous presence and combination of horizontal and vertical in which the rows of houses are laid out along an irregular route to which the skyscrapers used for offices act as a counterpoint.

Located on a trapezoidal lot and standing on a two-storey-high base, the Twin Towers are 138 m (37 storeys) and 127 m (34 storeys) high respectively, and each has an area of 1400 m². Together, the skyscrapers house a total of 2500 offices and are linked by five transparent bridges at different levels. in fact the decision to insert the plant in the floors and ceilings has allowed the façades to be glazed in their entirety and provide a completely permeable filter between the internal space and the external environment. A contrast to their formal and structural

purity is provided by the opaque multifunctional platform, which comprises cinemas, shops, bars, garages and underground structures extending 30 m below ground level.

Natural light reaches the spaces underground through large skylights, from which the unexpected view of the skyscrapers, from the bottom up, inverts the strong sense of vertigo.

The two transparent "colossi" are close but do not touch. They have contrasting appearances and are set at an angle of 59° to each other. Visible from every side, they reveal different aspects depending on the point of view. The space that they bound allows light to pass through, framing the city from different perspectives and transforming them into a metropolitan landmark that reinforces an established territorial tradition and at the same time provides a new area of expansion for the contemporary city.

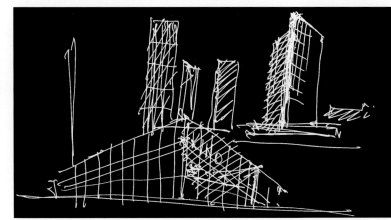

5. *Study sketch*

6-7. *Conceptual model and definitive model*

9-10. *The towers in relation to their surroundings. The podium as urban filter*

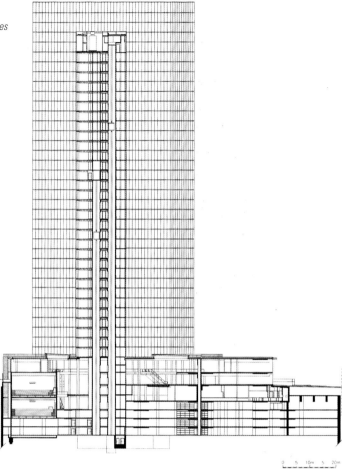

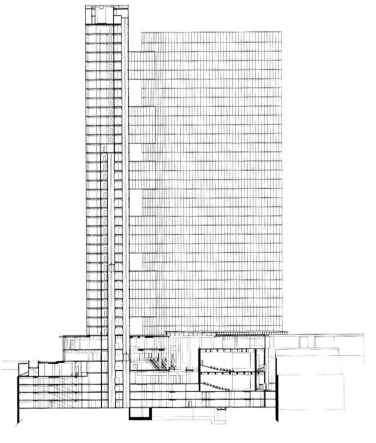

15. *Detail of the hall*

14. *Detail of the connections between the commercial podium and the towers*

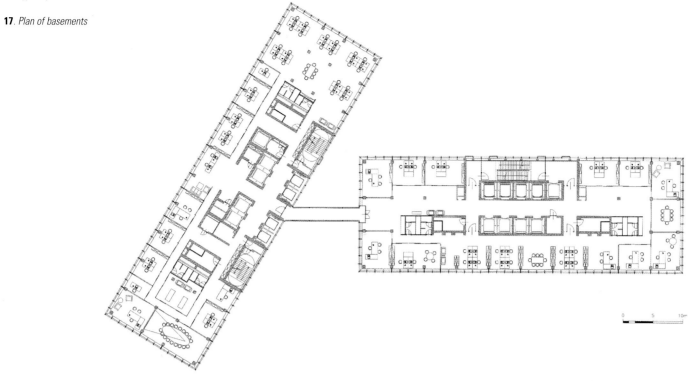

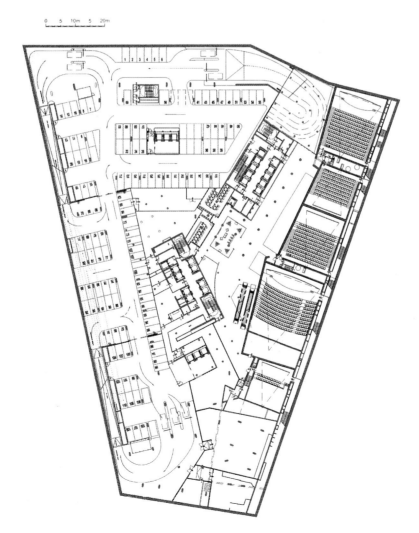

18-19. *The towers in relation to the west directrix of Vienna*

Europark 1, Salzburg (Austria)

The Europark in Salzburg covers an area of 120,000 m^2 situated in the vicinity of the motorway and the airport, to be used for commercial activities and a car park for 3000 auto.

The construction of this enormous complex was entrusted to Massimiliano Fuksas as the winner of an international competition held in 1994 for the development of a lot owned by the Spar Warenhandela AG, extended with subsequent interventions on behalf of Europark Errichtungsges m.b.H. The entertainment centre envisaged by the first programme is laid out on four levels, of which the ground floor and first floor house 80 shops, while basement and roof are both used as car parks, for 1200 and 600 vehicles respectively.

The building is clad on the outside by a double skin of blue glass, on both sides of which the back-lit logo "Europark" is silk-screened in white. The translucent surface of the façade changes with variations in the intensity of the light, further modified by the water that surrounds the whole perimeter and reflects and multiplies its image. The effect is noticeable even inside the megastore, where natural light penetrates easily, channelled by the inclined panes of glass of the large skylights and creating an ideal environment to enjoy the rest areas. A distinctive element of the design is the undulating roof that runs the whole length of the structure. Light and fluid, it echoes the movement of the waves of the sea which inspired it. Made of wire mesh and measuring 140 x 320 m, the roof is a landmark able to impart continuity to the complex and provide shelter for the cars. The same type of research, sensitive to flows and transparencies and equally attentive to its role as a landmark in the surrounding panorama, can be found in Europark II Inseln.

The operation entails the enlargement of the shopping centre and the redesign of the entire area. The new structure is laid out on two floors and is made up of two glazed volumes traversed by two more curved blocks. The car park, in this case located on the top level, is covered by "red islands", which in the space stitched together by an organization into raised wooden areas, footpaths, gardens and conservatories become protagonists of the system, whose own precise presence contrasts with the uninterrupted fluidity of the sinusoidal roof.

1-2. *Study sketches*

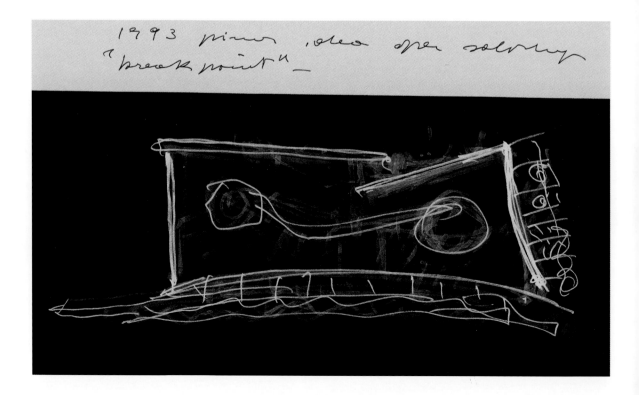

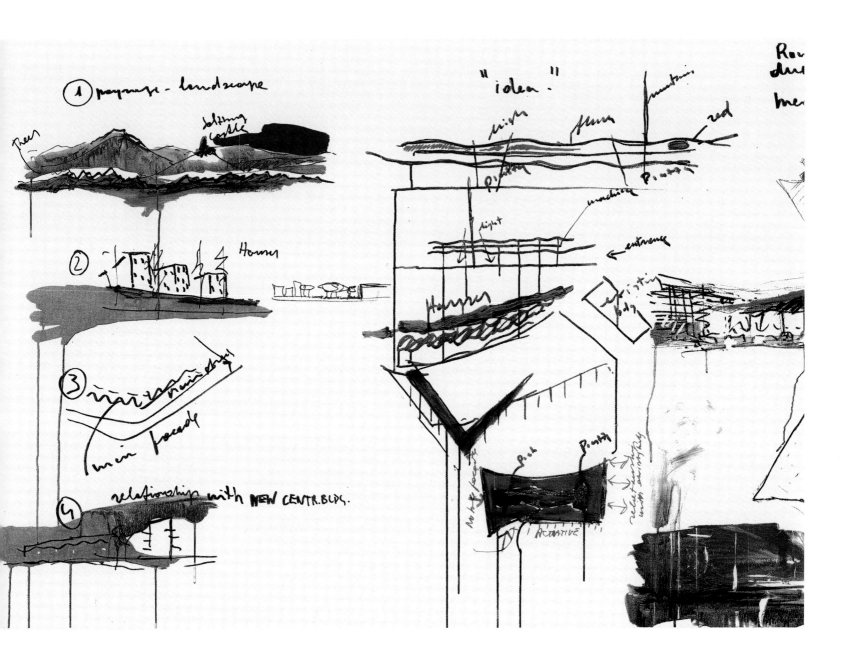

① paysage - landscape

② Horens

③ main facade

⑤ relationship with NEW CENTR.BLDS.

"idea"

entrance

Horens

3. *Elevations and longitudinal
and cross-sections*

4. *Study sketch*

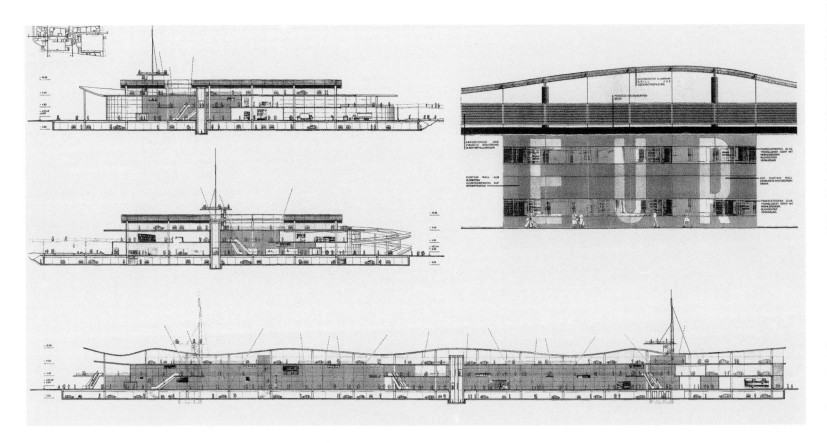

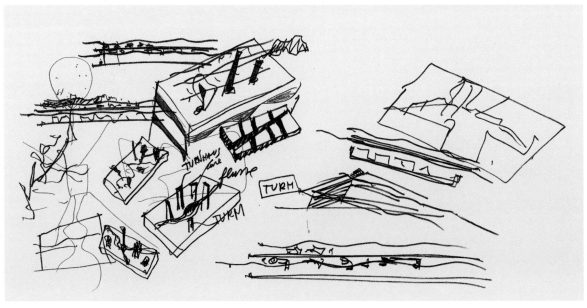

5. *General view. Stratigraphic relationship between the roofing of the elevated car park and the commercial structure*

6. *Night view of the roofing*   **7**. *View of the ramp*

Europark 2, Salzburg (Austria)

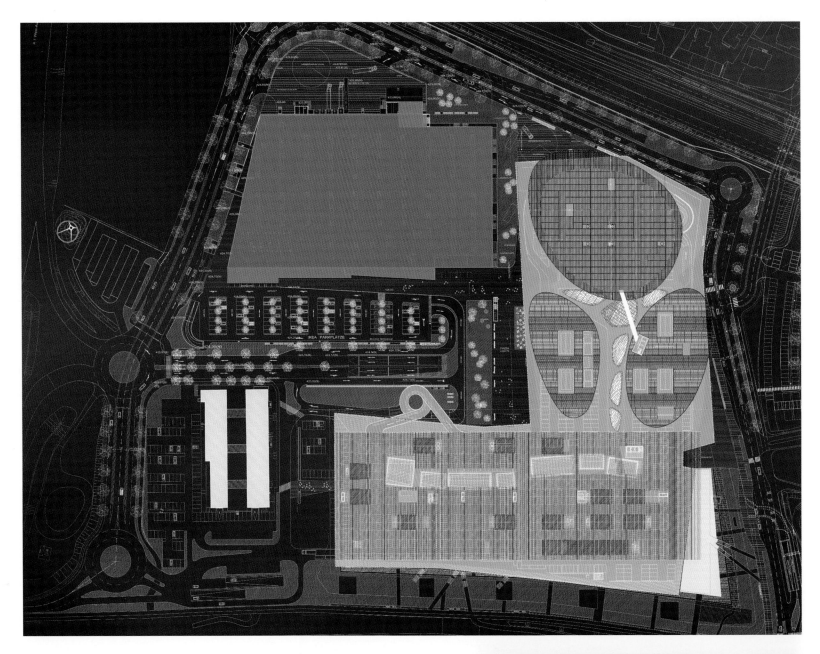

1. *Aerial view from south-east*

2. *General layout plan*

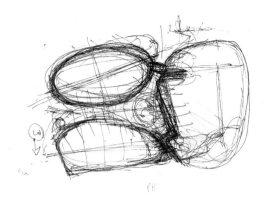

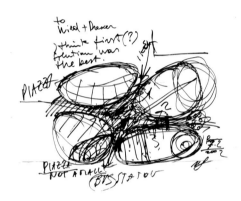

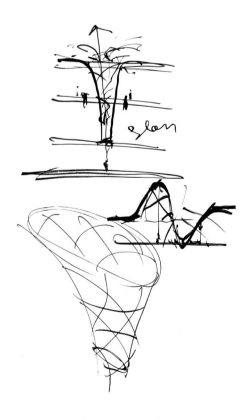

7. *Detail of the building under construction*

8. *General view of the construction site*

9. *Plan of the ground floor*

10. *Plan of the first floor*

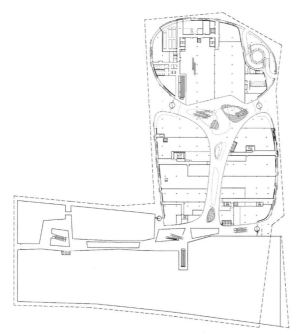

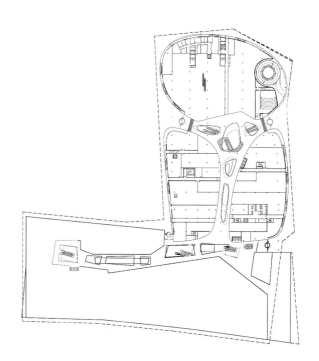

11. *Section*

12. *East elevation*

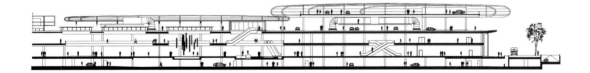

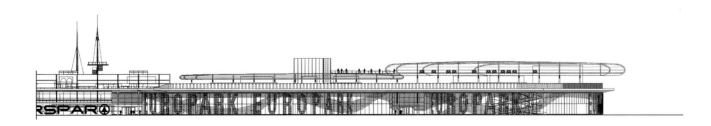

Maison des Arts, Bordeaux III (France)

1. *Maison des Arts, acrilico*

2. *View of the entrance*

3. *General view*

The Maison des Arts is the school of plastic and performing arts at the Michel de Montaigne University in Bordeaux.
A section of the university campus has been set aside for the complex. It is equipped with services, car parks and a large amount of free space for open-air activities connected with exceptional events and the everyday practice of the arts.
From the outset the project has been required to respond to the multiple needs of the specific subjects taught in the same structure, but has preserved its unitary character. in fact the institute comprises schools of drama, music, sculpture, radio and cinema that need particular settings for their courses as well as premises that do not limit the expression of individual talents. Fuksas has created an essential architecture that is able to adapt to any form of artistic expression, recognizing in spatial terms the independence of each disciplinary area without forgetting their mutual interaction.

The basic form is a parallelepiped traversed along its perimeter by a single fissure, interrupted by two large and vertical glazed openings that serve as entrances.
The construction has an internal complexity that is not apparent from the façade, clad in panels of pre-oxidized copper.
Only a detached and projecting block set on the roof interferes with the simple external disposition of masses. This is the broadcasting studio of Radio Campus, invisible from the inside and linked to the rest of the system by a glazed footbridge.
A slight break in the linearity of design is provided by the shutters of the windows and the contrasts of light and shade created by the holes that pierce the skin of the building at some points, revealing the interior.
The entrance to the school consists of a central atrium running the full height of the building which links the whole of the Primary School functionally as well as visually, serving as a foyer for the theatre

and exhibition hall and allowing both to maintain a clear autonomy in their schedules. Around the hall, the ground floor is occupied by the 350-seat auditorium with annexed rehearsal and cloakroom facilities and an exhibition area communicating with the studio of plastic arts. In the workshops brise-soleil screen the natural light that enters through the roof of the rooms devoted to graphics-printing, painting-colour and drawing, sculpture and decoration, which are flanked by an outdoor space for work in the open air.
The vestibule with a glass lift leads to the audiovisual and music departments on the first floor, laid out around a central corridor of communication between the various sectors. The one dedicated to music, composed of lecture halls for the courses, a media library and listening rooms, is located in the middle and separated at the sides by two empty spaces that ensure its soundproofing.

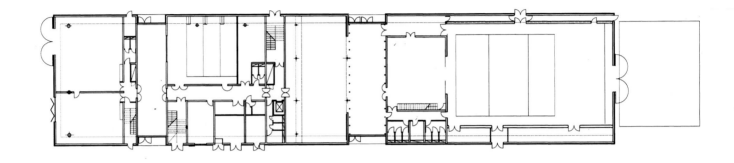

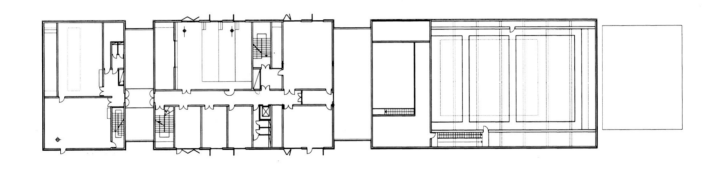

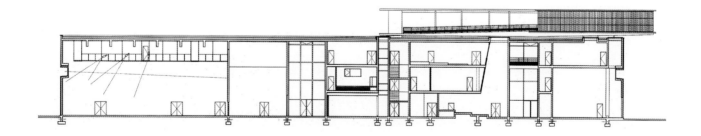

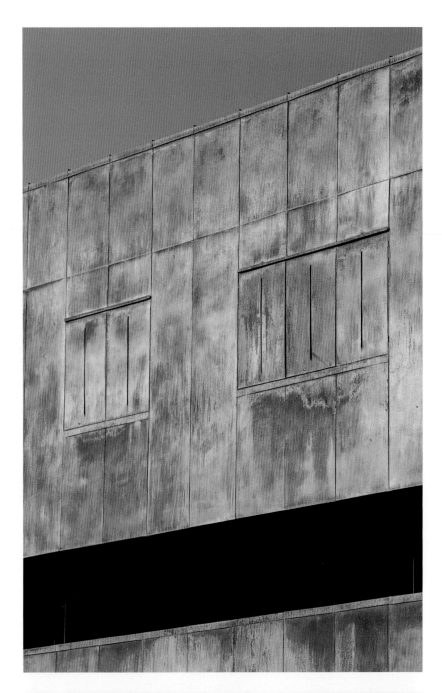

6. *Detail of the screened windows*

7. *Detail of the windows*

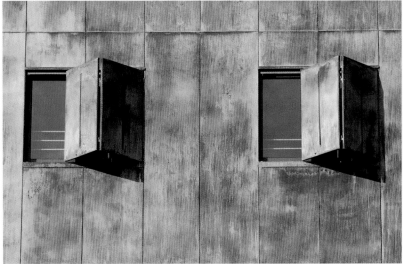

Competition for a synagogue, cultural centre and offices, Dresden (Germany)

1. *Model*

2. *Photo insertion*

The intervention is located in a historic area situated close to the mediaeval quarter of Dresden. The structure, intended to serve the local Jewish community, is in the vicinity of the ancient Carola Bridge that connects the original core of the city with its more recent expansion. The decision to allocate the funds for the new synagogue stems from the desire to give the religious body a worthy home to replace the one it had lost on Kristallnacht, between 9 and 10 November 1938.
The competition for the design of the complex was held in 1997, with a programme that required the insertion and rationalization of various facilities, including an auditorium, a library, a cultural centre and a school, in a total area of 3000 m². The proposed design houses all the functions in a single block which, in memory of the earlier complex built by Gottfried Semper that had been destroyed, is located on the same site. The building faces and extends towards the river Elba, with which it maintains a constant visual relationship even at a long distance. To the east, the old berth for boats becomes the natural reference for the pedestrian routes that connect with the rest areas along the Uferpromenade. The link established with the water in this way defines a renewed identity for the place, already perceptible at the entrance to the historic city.
Externally, the synagogue presents the appearance of a cube set immediately above water level on the platform of the "Brühlschen Terrasse". The base is marked by two incisive cuts made in the slab, which house commemorative sources of light, turned on the façade.

The configuration is the result of a superimposition of irregular layers of reinforced concrete and panes of glass of different intensities and transparencies that make up a façade in continual vibration. The alternating horizontal bands create a volume that is representative in its dimensions and significance, emerging from the surrounding fabric and distinguishing itself from it.
Thus the physical force conveyed by the construction becomes the emblem of a proven vocabulary of symbols able to represent the constancy and steadfastness of faith that has kept the Jewish people united over the centuries. Light is treated as an element capable of binding together and at the same time fragmenting the impressions conveyed in an effect amplified by the presence of the water.

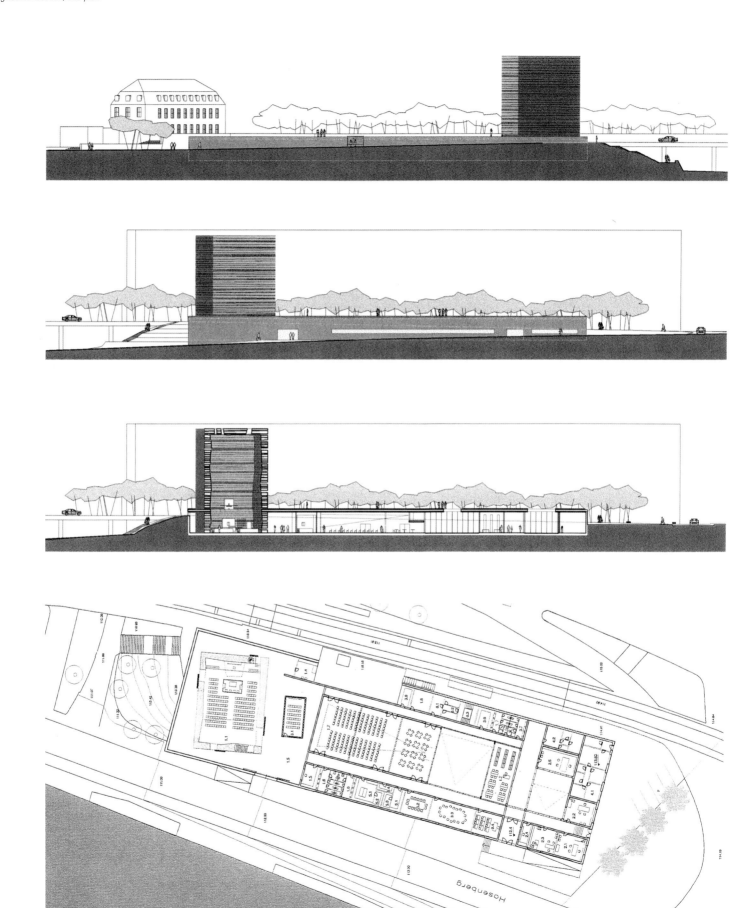

Peace Center, Jaffa (Israel)

The building of the Peres Center for Peace is specifically designed for its location in the Israeli city of Jaffa, situated at the end of the esplanade that runs from Tel Aviv. A seat with a highly representative character, a model of cooperation and dialogue, in one of the few areas in the world where different groups of the population with their respective ethnic, cultural and religious ties live together in peace.

The Peace Center represents an ideal and concrete place in which to develop the programmes and research connected with the mission inspired by the Nobel Peace Prize winner Shimon Peres, a meeting space for all those involved in the attempt to turn the Middle East into a place where people can work together to establish peace

through economic cooperation and mutual interaction, operating independently but in parallel to the political peace process.

The commission for the work has entrusted to Massimiliano Fuksas in 1997 by the Peres Center for Peace and FIMAR Constructions S.p.A. and the design was presented to the public at the Venice Biennale in 2000, with a 7-m-high scale model fitted with computer stations and used as a reception centre for visitors.

The Peace Center is a parallelepiped with a usable area of 7000 m² designed to house the offices of the Peres Foundation, a library, a media library, an auditorium for 200 people, an exhibition hall, a park, a conference centre and public services. The building has six storeys, each with a height of about 3.4 m,

that stand on a base at whose ends are located the entrance to the car park for 60 vehicles and the entrance for people arriving on foot, which opens onto a large square. The volume takes its form from the superimposition and succession of layers of different material and shape, built from local stone and translucent glass and resting on a compact platform. The contrast between light and shade created by the sequence of different levels is particularly evident on the ground floor where the reception is located, but it produces a uniform appearance on the outside as well. Natural light penetrates the building in the daytime and fills it, while at night the internal lighting communicates the presence and activity of the centre on the outside.

1-2. *Models: front and longitudinal section*

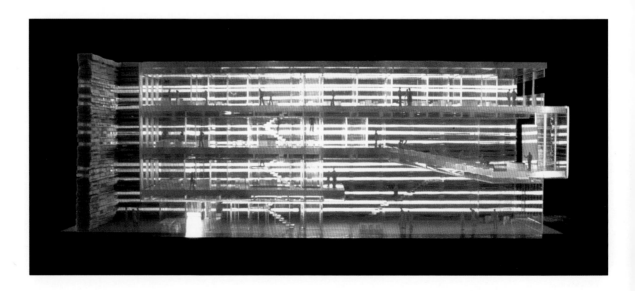

4. *Model*

5. *Study model, detail*

6. *Detail of the inside of the façade*

7. *Venice Biennale 2000, Pavilion of Peace,
scale model used for public presentation
of the project*

New Clothing Pavilion at Porta Palazzo, Turin (Italy)

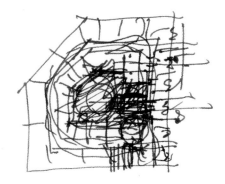

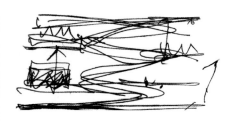

1-2. *Study sketches*

The area of Porta Palazzo in Turin, one of the oldest parts of the city, is an enormous open-air market situated close to archaeological sites and buildings designed by Juvarra and a short distance from the castle and cathedral. It used to be the entrance to the capital and is now the seat of numerous commercial activities that have transformed it over the course of time into a magnet for a heterogeneous community. The zone has an area of about 50,000 m^2 and has been the subject of a Plan of Urban Redevelopment approved and financed by the European Union together with the municipality of Turin and the Ministry of Public Works. An international competition then awarded Massimilano Fuksas the commission for the design of a new pavilion for clothing in the sector at the junction between Corso Regina Margherita and Corso Giulio Cesare.

The Roman architect's response is a glass-and-metal structure designed to house services and shops with a main entrance to the south-east, in the vicinity of Piazza della Repubblica, that holds a dialogue with the old underground ice-houses found on the site. On the ground floor, in fact, the area allocated to shops and bars is distributed along the outer edge of the building in order to leave the central space free and allow the historic relics to be seen.
The same planimetric scheme is used on the second level, where the commercial premises are served by a circular gallery from which run a series of ramps that span the void from one end to the other, leading to the refreshment area and the terrace. Light penetrates through slits in the metal roofing; resting on tapering pillars, this replicates the traces below, generated all the way from the basement levels. The

building has two underground levels, that of the car park with places for 109 vehicles and the one used for the technological plant, both of them conditioned by the presence of the wall around the archaeological excavation.
The whole building is enveloped by a double façade, with the fire escapes located in the space in between. Inside the wall of masonry unifies the structure, which on the outside appears to be clad in a series of glass planes held by pairs of steel uprights. The entranceway, rendered unique by the work of the artist Mimmo Paladino, who has inserted sculptural elements made of iron, opens onto the part at the base where metal is assigned a greater role with respect to the transparent surface, perfecting the refined contamination between art and architecture that underpins the whole project.

3. *Urban plan*

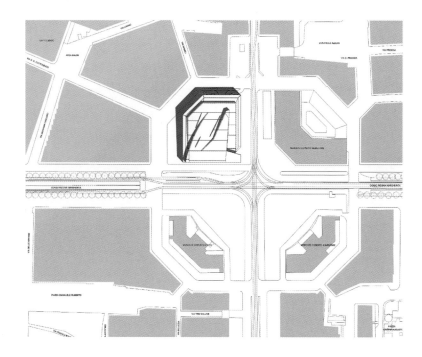

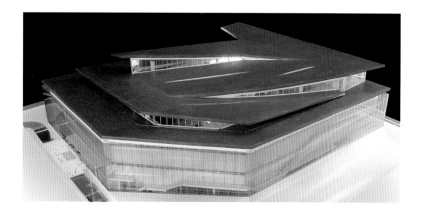

6. *General view: the relationship between the new pavilion and the existing commercial structures*

7. *Study sketch*

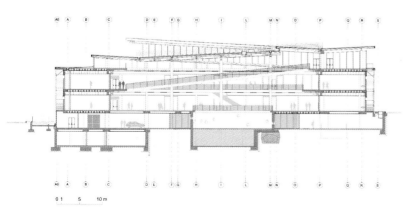

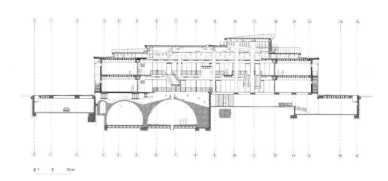

10. *The façade as strata of matter and light: night-time view*

11. *Sketch by Mimmo Paladino: the inserts in the façade*

12. *The relationship between the multilayered glass façade and the internal structure of reinforced concrete: details*

13. *Sketch by Mimmo Paladino: detail of the inserts*

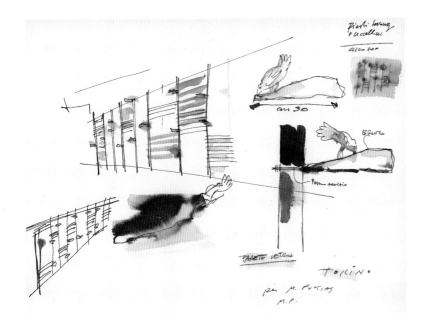

On following pages

14. *The footbridges and the internal vertical connections: detail from the construction site*

15. *The new roofing and the historic city*

1. *Study sketch*

2. *Model: the entrance*

3. *Model, view of the interior*

The project is located on a lot of about 2000 m^2 in a recently developed district adjacent to the North Ring Road envisaged by the new town plan drawn up by the municipality of Foligno.

The complex has been commissioned by the Italian Episcopal Conference through the diocese in which the Fuksas Studio, winner of the related competition, is located.

At the base of the programme is proposed the construction of two volumes with a total area of around 1500 m^2, allocated respectively to the church and to the other activities of the institute, including a reception centre, the sacristy and the canon's house. Both blocks take the form of parallelepipeds, linked together by a structure in satin glass comprising the Ferial Chapel. The first block, for the church, is taller, while the other, lower block, measures 60 x 12 m and has two storeys, taking it to a height of about 7 m. The remaining free area is given over entirely to vegetation and, at the rear, car parks and playing fields with facilities.

In front of the church is laid out the parvis, which gives onto the new link road to the ring road. The square emphasizes the entrance to the parish church, a sharp horizontal slash set about a metre above the ground, which runs right across the front and is accessible by means of a footbridge. The church has an area of about 30 x 22.5 m and a height of 25 m, and is the product of the intersection of two parallelepipeds, one comprised within the other to form a nave and two aisles. The outer one is built of reinforced concrete treated with wax and the smaller and inner one of lightweight cellular concrete.

A series of holes made in the surfaces lets in natural light, which passes through the double structure and is directed towards the main elements of the hall, conveyed by hollow structural chains that, linking the two walls, give material form to the rays of sunlight and lend centrality to the altar. The perception of the internal space is also modified by the work of the artist Maurizio Nannucci. Iridescent quotations from the Gospels run along the walls, triggering a stimulating pattern of artificial lights that blends with the illumination from the sides and from the skylights in the ceiling.

4. *Study sketches: relationship between inside and outside*

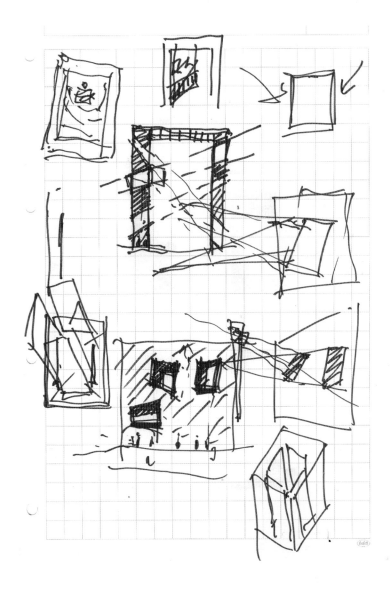

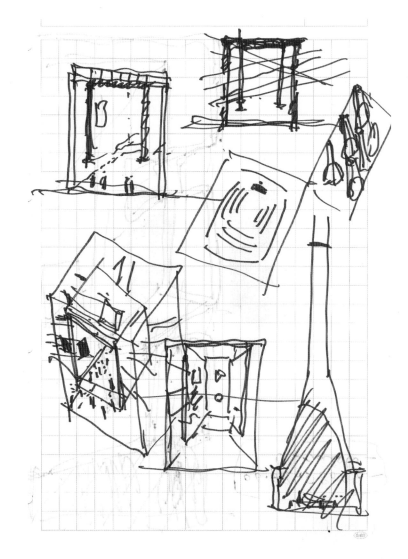

Hansforum and Alsterfleet, Hamburg (Germany)

Both the complexes located in Hamburg, on the bank of the Alsterfleet and near the Axel-Springer Platz respectively, are intended for offices. The former is an intervention on the last lot of a historic quarter situated between the old part of the city to the east and the modern expansion to the west; the latter is set at the junction of the square with a very busy main road onto which the principal block faces.

In both cases the Fuksas Studio has sought to create an effect of maximum transparency and appropriation of the context that allows the new spaces to be perceived as a natural extension of the geography outside.

Along the course of the Alster the complex of constructions – office block and residential buildings – is raised one level above the quays by means of tall pillars that allow free passage. Lined up along an east-west axis, they follow the course of the pedestrian area, treated as a scenic route in close contact with the water.

The building at the southern end has a large entrance hall and is laid out around a central spine of connections and services. It is clad entirely with a double shell of glass and regulates its microclimate by interacting with the sunlight, creating a pleasant working atmosphere inside.

In fact natural light serves all the units on the six upper floors, which offer views of the city and the nearby port. The construction is integrated with the surroundings by means of the translucent façade, characterized chromatically by the insertion of a green film. The appearance and transparency of the building change, influenced by the illumination and the reflections from the water, turning the object into a living organism.

The link with the surroundings is also emphasized in the flats which, faced with brick and apparently more introverted, have large glazed openings on the side extending towards the river, with which they seek to establish constant visual contact. In this way, the configurations become the product of an uninterrupted exchange of light, images and movements between nature and artificial elements.

With the Hanseforum too the intention was to shape a fluid space capable of holding a dialogue with the surroundings. The project proposed the creation of a covered plaza at the junction of two streets, as a link between two seven-storey office blocks, contrasting strongly in form and conception. The two blocks, one characterized by gleaming ceramic balustrades and the other completely glazed, are unified from the formal and functional point of view into a single system. The entrance hall becomes the pivot of the new organization in which each block is linked to the next through a series of bridges and staircases; an area devoted to shops and restaurants, its temperature regulated by means of natural light and the heat stored by the buildings. It is a construction composed of transparencies and structures left open to view, light and glazed in its entirety, which allows the sky and the city to enter, becoming part of them.

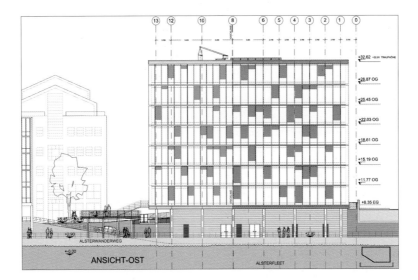

1. *Hansforum: side elevation*

2. *Hansforum, general view of the new intervention in relationship to the canal and the city*

3-5. *Residential buildings, cross-sections and longitudinal section*

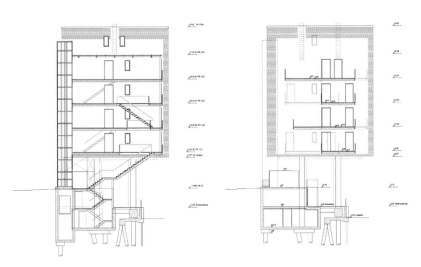
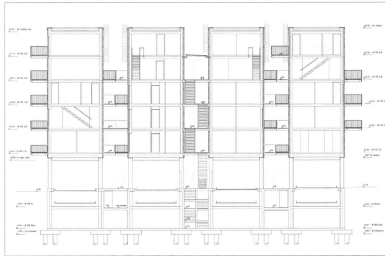

6. *Residential buildings, general view*

7. *Residential buildings, head block*

8. Hansforum, office building

9. Hansforum, office building, cross section

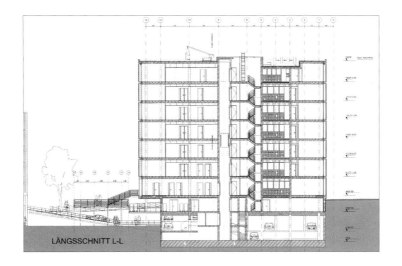

LÄNGSSCHNITT L-L

131

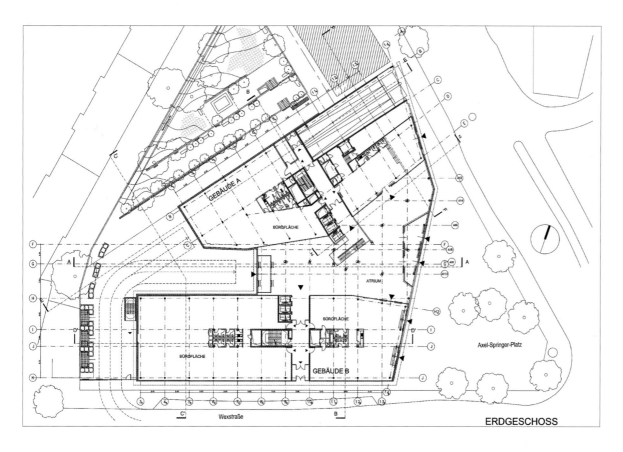

ERDGESCHOSS

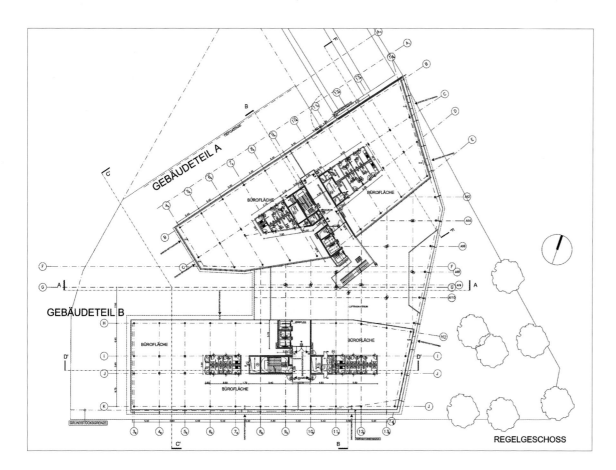

REGELGESCHOSS

12. *Alsterfleet, general view, the street,
the hall and the offices*

13. *View of the roofing*　　　　**14**. *View of the stairs*

Palazzo Centro Congressi EUR, Rome (Italy)

The Congress Centre will stand alongside the Torri delle Finanze, on a site of 27,000 m^2 in the EUR district comprised between the axes of Viale Europa, Viale Colombo, Viale Asia and Viale Shakespeare. Along with the existing building, the new centre will become the hub of the system of conference facilities in the area, responding to the requirements laid down in the programme of the competition held by the municipality of Rome with the intention of improving the international image of the capital.

In 1998 the first prize in this international competition went to the project submitted by the Fuksas Studio: a structure of 58,000 m^2 designed to accommodate over 10,000 people, which will include a 1800-seat auditorium, two conference halls measuring 5000 and 3000 m^2 respectively that can be used alternatively for temporary exhibitions and a 600-room hotel, all equipped with services and connections. A programme that also called for facilities to provide a direct shuttle service between the complex and car parks with a capacity of 2500 vehicles. The system is organized around a translucent parallelepiped: set longitudinally, it is 75 m wide, 198 m long and 30 m high and opens at the sides onto two squares conceived as places of rest and interaction. Both are in direct contact with the district and serve as spaces for the reception and distribution of users. Their function is to facilitate the integration of the complex into the city and draw in a broader swathe of the public to see the works of art on display. The simplicity of the outer casing echoes the linearity of the historic fabric of the EUR, linked to the rationalist architecture of the 1930s and the existing Congress Centre designed by Adalberto Libera. The cloud, a totally free form in which the conference halls will be housed, is the distinguishing sign of the intervention. It will appear to be suspended inside the shell, halfway between the floor and the ceiling of the large illuminated hall. Built out of steel and Teflon, it will be supported by a dense mesh of steel ribs, braced and resting on three elements.

Its appearance seems to shift with the point of view, changing continually, and the caged cloud looks as if it were floating on a current of air.

1. *Site plan*

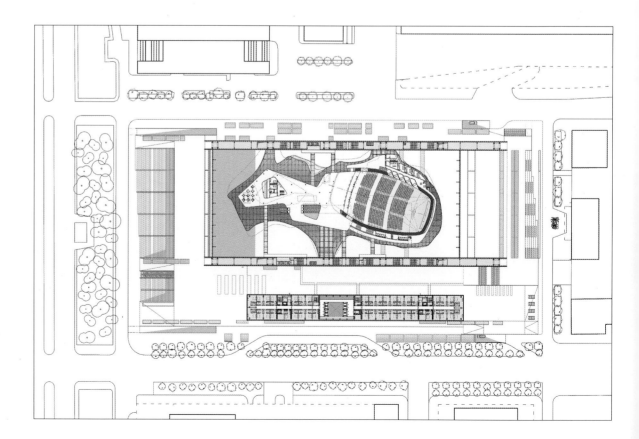

2. *The cloud: acrylic on plastic, 1998*

On following pages:
3. *The cloud and the container: virtual
simulations*

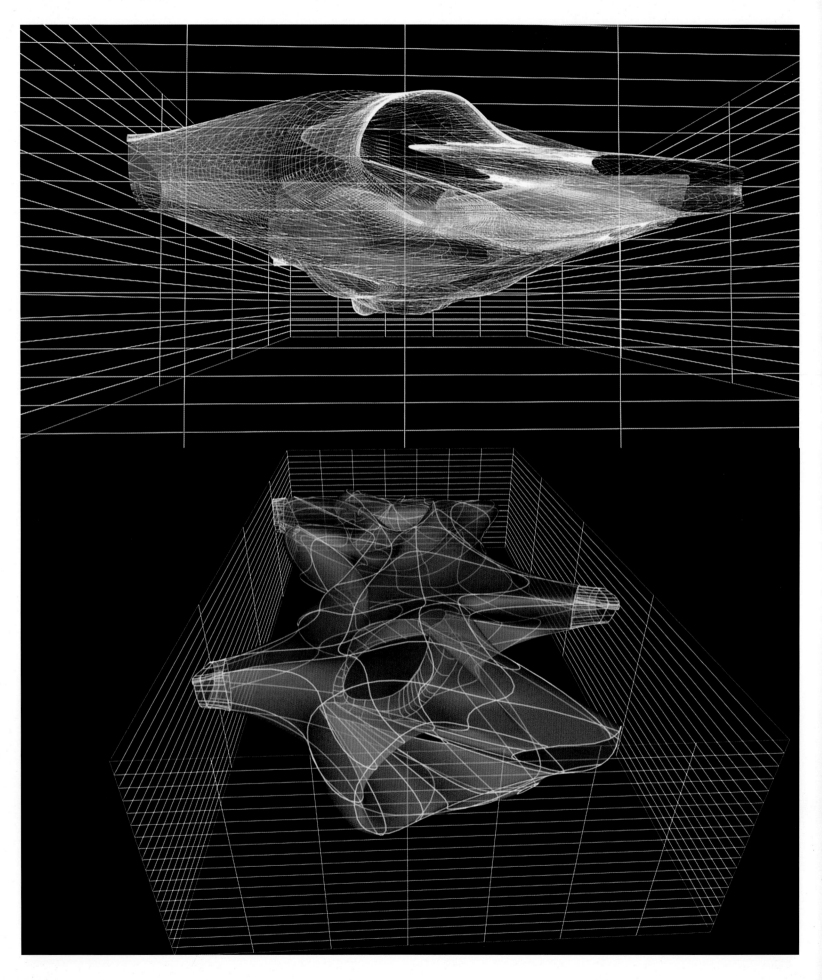

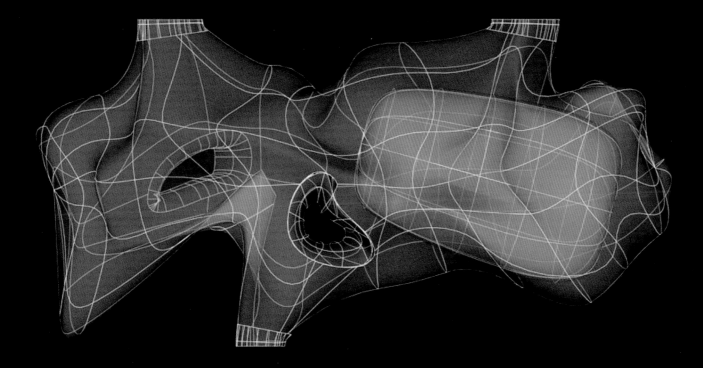

4. *Model*

5. *Cross section*

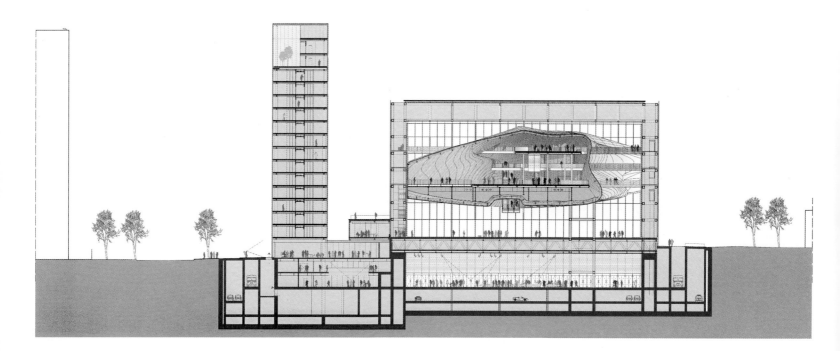

6. *Perspective: the cloud in relationship to the box of the Conference Centre*

7. *Cross-section*

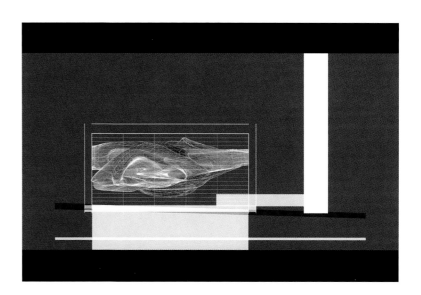

Conversation with Walter Veltroni and Massimiliano Fuksas, Palazzo del Campidoglio, Rome, April 2005

This project has a long and complicated history, but what does the Conference Centre represent at this moment as far as a policy for the city of Rome is concerned?

Veltroni: I will tackle this question from three points of view.

The first regards the city's economy, and seen from this point of view the Conference Centre is strategic. Today Rome is obtaining excellent results from tourism. This is largely the result of two factors: on the hand the cultural life of the city and on the other its safety, with the indisputable base of its beauty... as *sine qua non*. What is lacking in Rome, however, and which has now started to develop with Renzo Piano's Auditorium, but which should be there on a quite different scale when the new Conference Centre is built, is the dimension of conference tourism, which could have enormous repercussions on the structure of the city's economy.

The second aspect, for those of us who have an almost obsessive interest in attaining the objective, is that with the choice of a Conference Centre designed by Massimiliano Fuksas we are trying to bring an emblem of contemporary architecture back to Rome after forty-five years of silence.

The last great examples were the ones designed by Nervi, followed by decades in which there was no great architecture of quality. So our goal is to have a series of great works of contemporary architecture in Rome.

At this moment, in addition to Fuksas's work, we have Renzo Piano who has designed the Auditorium, Odile Decq who is building the Macro, Zaha Hadid with the MAXXI, Rem Koolhaas who is designing the new Mercati Generali, Richard Meier with the church at Tor Tre Teste and the Ara Pacis, Paolo Portoghesi who is building another auditorium, Vittorio Gregotti who is working on a new residential and service centre at Acivia, Richard Rogers who is planning a new district at Magliana; in short, we again have ten or so great works by architects from Italy and elsewhere, which are going to leave an important mark on the city.

The third and from my point of view most important element concerns the design itself. In other words you can build a conference centre but Fuksas has designed "the conference centre", with a symbol that is the symbol of the city. I really like the idea of the cloud, because it is the representation of the city as I would like it to be and of the city as it to a great extent is. A light and elegant, functional and modern sign, but one that does not lose that characteristic of beauty which is to be found in this city, and not only on the Capitol. Really. And this architectural sign that Massimiliano Fuksas has chosen is even better suited to the city that we have. So from my point of view our task is to make sure that it is built as soon as possible. We are now on the home straight, and it is a priority goal since I consider it one of the symbols of the new Rome.

From this viewpoint, and bearing in mind the difficult experience of the construction of the Auditorium in recent years, how will the city council of Rome tackle the operation of this complex machinery? On what time scale, with what sort of schedule? For with the great rivalry between the great cities of the world in the construction of major works a lot rides on things like efficiency, keeping to schedule and high quality of execution.

Veltroni: To clarify this point I will take just one other example. We are now planning to build three schools of quality on the outskirts of Rome after a big international competition. This means changing our way of thinking about the city, moving from an intensive logic to one of quality, without this bringing us into conflict with the quantitative dimension. In other words we need to do many things, but we need to do many things well. It is no longer possible for us to make ugly things. For the administration making lots of beautiful things signifies raising the threshold of attention to the aspect of quality, and reorganizing the machinery as well. In the case of the Conference Centre the thing that has made everything a bit more complicated is the fact that the design has come out of a competition held by an external body, the EUR, and not directly by the municipality. And only one client with a single contractor has submitted a tender. Now we are working with this contractor to ensure that the deadlines are met. We want the work to start between the end of this year and the beginning of the next. We will have done all that we could.

Well that shows that there is a real political will here, that contemporary architecture has become part of the agenda of the public administration.
Veltroni: Look, I have learned something in these days [the funeral of Pope John Paul II, *author's note*], that there is nothing you cannot do if you want to do it. When a politician, an administrator, says that something cannot be done, it means that he doesn't want to do it.

In these first reflections we have spoken mainly of major public works, so what does it mean to design a communal space today?
Veltroni: Let's take the example of schools... We already have a good stock of schools. Many of them date from the late 19th century and the early decades of the 20th and so were designed for the needs of students in that period of history. Now the needs, the desires have completely changed: computers, sport, colours, everything is different. The idea of the forms is different.

What we are doing in the case of schools today is to try to put together an investigation of what are the desires of students, and of children too, because setting up a nursery school today is quite a different thing from thirty years ago. It's the idea that architecture is not just a symbol but a project, a project of life, of civil organization. It is a social project.

The civil responsibility of architecture is that generations of people will pass through the building for years. It will influence their lives, the ways they perceive space.
Fuksas: Now we have a reaffirmation of the fact that the city needs architecture and commissions of architecture. I think that reasserting the role of commissions in this city is a very important thing.

It is a fundamental realization.
Veltroni: Paradoxically, if I have to build something, it's no longer enough to say that I'll hold a competition. It's what happens before the competition that has become crucial, the idea that you ask the architect to put into effect which already has to be organized in a new way with respect to the past. And the commission cannot be a commission understood solely in terms of exclusivity and political responsibility. It entails a social relationship, a type of relationship that you then bring into play with the user of the architecture, which is decisive.

So what type of architecture is the centre?
Fuksas: The architecture of the Conference Centre in Rome was my dream, that of building in Rome. Now that I have extricated myself from the Milan Trade Fair I am going to be closely connected with the Conference Centre. The problem for me was building in Rome. I hope to do other works, but for me the Conference Centre comes first. It's the most important work of my life. It's a project that has been going on for seven years and I'm not bored with it. It's a very difficult project to carry out, not for the architecture but above all for the structure. For me it's the synthesis of all that there is in Rome, it's my desire to be part of this city which owes so much to the world of Borromini, the baroque city. The whole of our city is like a great sculpture and it's a great sculpture that is contained in a lightness. And then on the other hand there is the respect for this world, which is not just the culture between the two wars, Roman rationalism, but Palazzo Farnese too. The parallelepiped, the case that contains it, is Renaissance and anti-Renaissance, classical and anti-classical, and this is a bit the world. Rome is beautiful because it feeds on the contradiction between classical and anti-classical if it were just baroque.

It's a strong box that contains an act of great wonder. What emotions do you want it to express? What do want the visitor to feel entering the Conference Centre?

Veltroni: I'm sure that it will be a sensation of lightness, which for me is the most important thing in life. The sense that Calvino gave to this word. In *American Lessons* Calvino said: *your modernity is a graveyard of rusty machinery*. In the times in which we live lightness is an absolute cultural value. I think that anyone entering it will have this sensation, contrasting with everything that is proposed to them from outside, from the world of television represented by the programme "Isola dei Famosi".

I think that the city still has to give shape to new monuments...

Veltroni: It's history, what has remained and what has gone against time, not what has gone in time. Going against time means: I hope to anticipate it! Or to have a testimony to the best there is... and there's no doubt that having a light work of architecture in a world like that of today is a revolution.

Fuksas: There is the expectation of the people who ask me about the cloud in the street.

I believe it is very important for architecture to go back to being a shared collective element.

Veltroni: This is Rome... and Massimiliano Fuksas's design. I've been to the Guggenheim but I don't remember any of the works that were on show there because of the overpowering presence of the architecture. But the design of the Conference Centre is absolutely functional... It is a very grand idea in a context of functionality and respect for the nature of the design and the object, and even after seven years this makes it up-to-date and eagerly awaited... even more so.

One last question. Fuksas's work in these years is proving that it is possible to produce architecture of a very high level in Italy, and this is a very strong signal for Italian architecture, which shows that Italian architecture is emerging from a long phase of decadence. What does an administrator expect from the Italian architecture of the next few years? From the young? What can you ask for?

Veltroni: The most banal answer is imagination. But it is banal. Because if we take Fuksas's design, it's not just a highly imaginative idea but very rational too, and it's characteristic of the place, it's historically determined. Imagination is not enough. An interpretation of the social, historical context is needed. The greatness of Italy lies in the fact that we are a talented and cultured country. We cannot be just one or the other, because either we will turn into an America that we are not capable of being if we're just talented, or we will become a museum if we are just cultured. We have to be both things at once. That is what I would ask from Italian architecture.

Listening to the heart of the city again.

Veltroni: Yes, but also having a taste for the before and after, for looking at the sides, for seeing the context, for attending to society and not just the project, for every project has a social effect that is part of the project.

Being realistically visionary.

Veltroni: Which is the only way to live.

The project is conceived for the disused military area of the Montello barracks, situated in the vicinity of the Olympic Village and the Flaminio Stadium in Rome. In 2000 the Fuksas Studio won an international competition staged by the Italian Space Agency (ASI) for its new headquarters, with the scientific coordination of La Sapienza University. The ASI building is located on the lot marked out by Via Masaccio and Via Guido Reni in a district that is defining its identity around a series of high- quality interventions by well-known contemporary architects. The proposed building is set at right angles to the two streets, favouring the longitudinal axis along the Via Flaminia that permits the construction to align itself with the church and the existing screen of buildings. The chosen disposition leaves free a broad strip of land to be planted with vegetation. This green corridor is designed to serve, in fact, as a direct visual connection between the headquarters of the space agency and the future Centre for the Contemporary Arts (MAXXI) designed by Zaha Hadid for the same area in 1998 The complex presents the pure appearance of a translucent and semi-transparent parallelepiped that reveals its internal flows and arrangements, traversed by a curvilinear form that floats in space, threading the six floors destined for offices and the two underground levels of the car park. The entrance is located on the ground floor where an atrium serves to direct visitors along different routes from the ones reserved for the staff. The most regular part, set aside for the offices of the administration, management and director, is totally autonomous and connected with the exhibition sector by a central strip devoted to support services and areas of interchange between the different sections. The public will follow the concave-convex course of the double strip which, as it bends, creates a series of spaces destined for a museum of the evolution of the sciences, a multimedia auditorium and a cafeteria.

Light is reflected along the transparent surface that envelops the construction, multiplied *ad infinitum* at every curve in the sinusoid. The impression is reinforced by the installation of an enormous liquid-crystal screen, used as a substitute for the façade and providing the true connection with the city.

1-2. *Study sketches*

3-4. *Plans and sections*

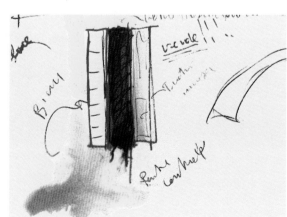

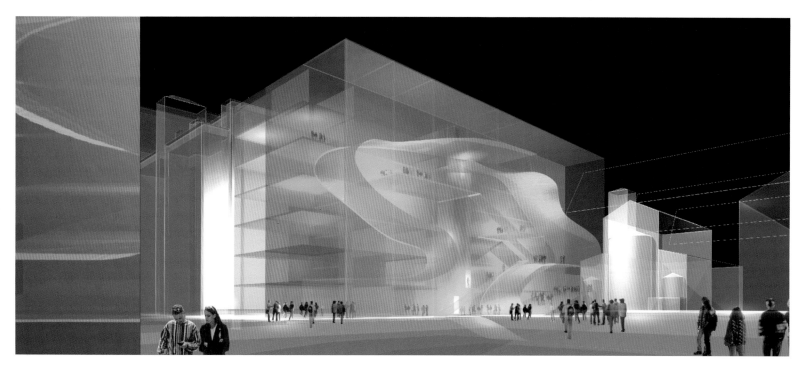

concorso europeo di progettazione

la nuova sede dell'agenzia spaziale italiana

piano primo

piano secondo

piano terzo

sezione longitudinale B-B   1:200

sezione trasversale C-C   1:200

11-05-2000

147

Mall and casino extension, Eindhoven (Netherlands)

1. *Study sketch*

2. *Master plan*

3. *Prospect, insertion in the context*

4. *View of the gallery from inside the new intervention*

The area is located between the central station and the commercial zone of Eindhoven, situated in a vital position with respect to the historic part of the Dutch city. The operation has been carried out on a site characterized in the past by the incisive presence of the shopping facilities in which the project is required to intervene, including a supermarket rebuilt in the 1970s and the De Bijenkorf department store, an important work by Giò Ponti dating from 1967.

In 1998 the municipality of Eindhoven held an international competition for the redefinition of the central belt of the city. The Fuksas Studio won and drew up the masterplan, committing itself, from that moment on, to the realization of the ideas proposed, a process that is now nearing completion.

The plan set out to give a greater stimulus to the urban centre, providing it with additional commercial axes that will also function as a link between the main sectors of the built-up area. Fuksas has imagined an entrance formed by department stores and two 15-m-high glass bubbles, the Admirant and the restaurant-casino, one located on each of the accesses to the new "September 18" Square.

Onto the redesigned space face the Shopping Mall Piazza, with an area of around 20,000 m², and 6000 m² of office space created by the renovation and extension of the existing construction, which has been connected with Bridges' building and a Media Market covering 8000 m². A pedestrian route leads right into the piazza, forcefully underlining the north-south axis characterized by a transparent roof set on 25-m-high Cor-Ten pillars shaped to a design by the artist Massimo Mazzonc. The system embraces the Bijenkorf respectfully, almost without any material contact, asserting its monumental presence in the visual field of the department store, filtered solely by the all-glass façade. The translucent casing takes on a green colouring on the lower floors and envelops the whole of the shopping centre, linking up by means of a bridge with the adjacent electronics shop, faced with blue ceramic tiles.

The same effect of fluid interpenetration is produced between the different levels of the shopping centre, redesigned through the creation of enormous elliptical gashes in the floors that allow natural light to penetrate from above and unify the various sections of the mall in all directions. Moving in the opposite direction, the illumination of the parking lot for 2000 bicycles located under the piazza is visible on the outside through transparent panels set in the paving.

Accessibility and convergence between the parts are the factors that shape the whole of the project for "September 18" Square, which succeeds in making it easier to cross and turning it back into a pleasant place for a stroll, sparking off a continual exchange that does not admit gaps and hidden objects.

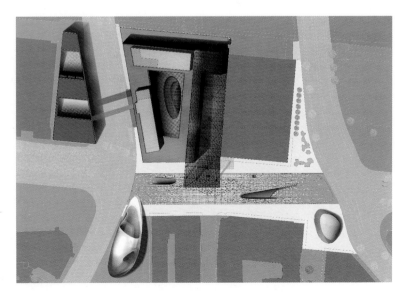

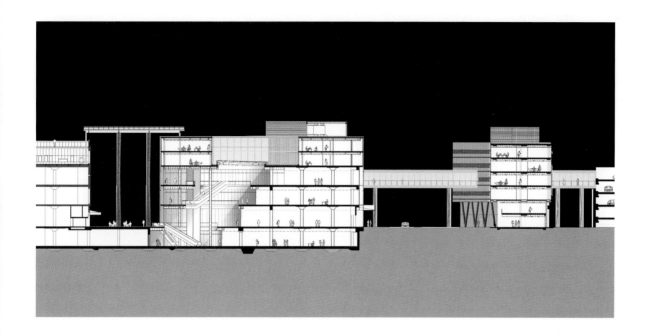

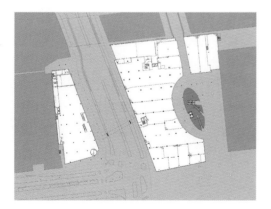 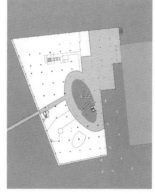 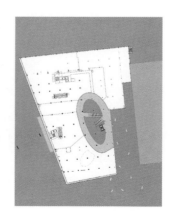

13. *View of the central space*

14. *Detail of the pillars*

15. *Detail of the commercial fronts*

16. *The ramp and the new intervention in relationship to Giò Ponti existing building*

17-18. *Simulations of the casino in relationship to the city*

19. *North section of the casino*

20. *Vertical section*

21. *Section of the cycle park*

22. *Detail of the cycle park*

23. *Longitudinal section of the bicycle park*

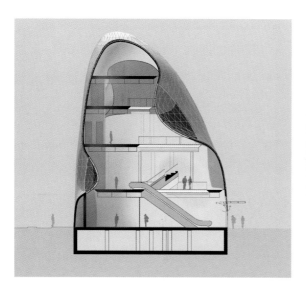

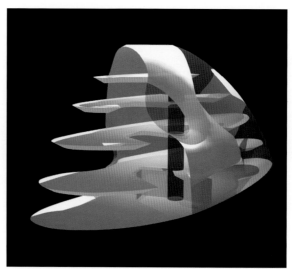

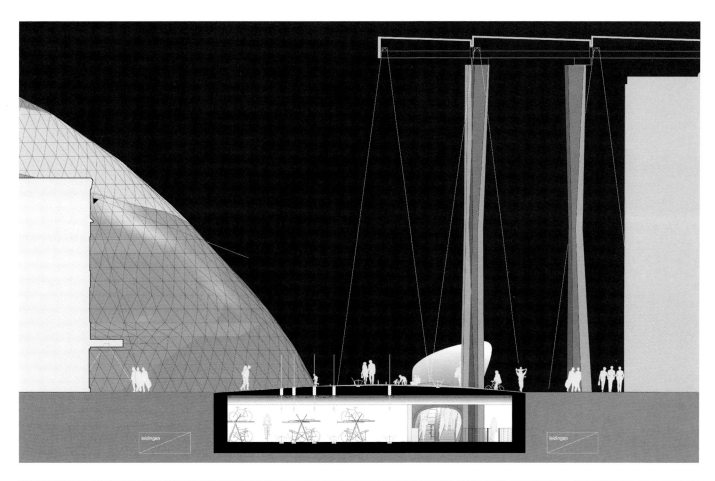

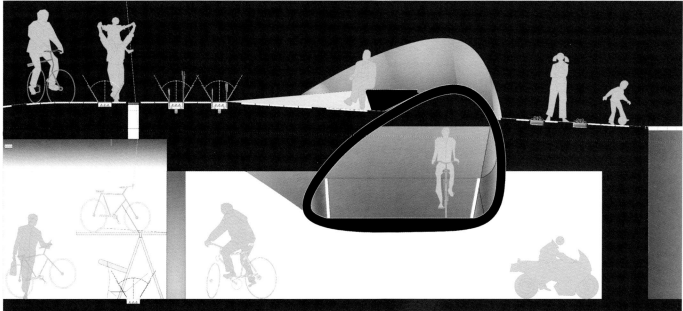

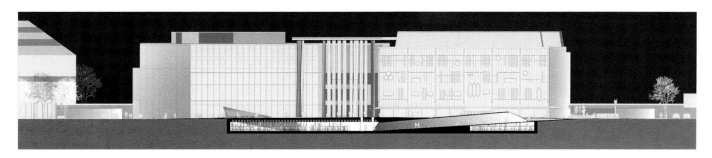

155

Competition for the new seat of regional government in Piedmont, the Palazzo della Regione Piemonte, Turin (Italy)

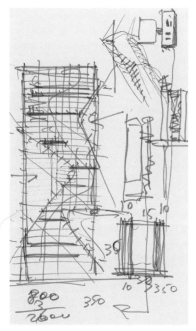

1. *Study sketch*

The area of intervention is situated in the vicinity of the branch railway line leading to France in one direction and Genoa/Porta Nuova in the other, and is an empty piece of land, free of constraints and ties with pre-existing built-up areas.

The project was commissioned by the Region of Piedmont from Massimiliano Fuksas after he won the international competition for the construction of a new seat of government. The regional authority's scheme is part of a broader plan for upgrading the area, in which it aims to act as a recognizable element, performing an effective symbolic role on a vaster scale. The lot assigned to the project, left free by the closure and subsequent dismantling of the Materferro works, owes its trapezoidal shape to the presence of the railway line. The building that will be constructed on it,

with a height of around 100 m, will provide an effective landmark in the built-up context set at the end of the north-south axis.

The complex consists of a thirty-storey-high tower housing the offices, a lateral 14.2-m-high volume used for a variety of functions and an underground car park with an area of 25,000 m².

The main block, glazed in its entirety, is divided into different sectors, all of them accessible from the entrance hall, which is organized on three levels to facilitate the distribution of users. The connection with the upper storeys is provided by stairs and lifts serving the various units. The position of the numerous offices varies considerably in relation to the location of the "blades" that run along one side of the building. Along the western strip, the transverse planes are free to modify their inclination

continually, contained within the "large void" that is set above the hall, unifying the space vertically.

On the same side is set the lower building, which houses a conference centre, bar and restaurant. Also glazed, it provides access to the rooms by means of a suspended passageway on the second level of the entrance hall or from the second underground floor. An area will be created between the two blocks to serve as a plaza, a meeting place to attract visitors and induce them to make use of the structure.

The project as a whole gives rise to a visually transparent organism that lets in light and the external surroundings and, at the same time, to an extroverted and permeable system that is open to people and the city.

2-3. *Models*

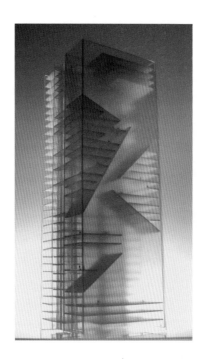

Ferrari operational headquarters, Maranello (Modena, Italy)

The new research centre of the famous Italian car manufacturer is located at Maranello, in the Ferrari citadel on the avenue that bears the name of its founder. In 2000 Ferrari S.p.A., engaged in a wider programme of consolidation of the group's image, decided to give Massimiliano Fuksas the job of designing its product development centre, allotting it an area of 17,000 m². The building, which will house the operations of the Ferrari Technical Management, is located on a strategically representative site at the centre of the campus and already subject to general changes for some time.

It is in this perspective that we must see the determination of the management to provide its employees with the most comfortable environmental conditions, through a comprehensive redesign of the various work areas.

Fuksas's proposal is to bring the element of "nature" into a place that has always been characterized by the most advanced technological research. The resulting image is inspired by the flatness of the Emilian countryside: a transparent volume, on which stands a block of glass that projects outwards for 7 m above the entrance and is reflected in the pools of water beneath. The Ferrari Research Centre is a calm and light structure of steel and glass, bound together visually by simple panes of glass, that relates to its surroundings by bringing them inside and by itself becoming part of them.

Access to the first floor is provided by lithe aluminium staircases located in the central courtyard and supported on slender reinforced-concrete pillars. Wooden footbridges run above the "water garden", creating a network of connections that leads to the meeting rooms. Both built of glass, these are characterized by the company's emblematic colours, yellow and red, which are also used along the internal routes. The reflections of the water and the shimmering of the light model the space and conceal the sloping plinths of black metal that support the construction, reinforcing the impression that the building is suspended over an almost enchanted landscape, peopled by bamboo and pebbles.

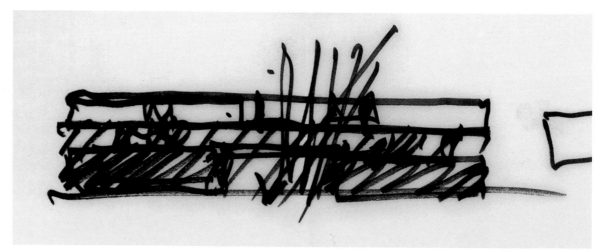

1-2. *Sketches: section and relationship with the natural light*

5. *Site plan*

6. *Axonometric vertical section*

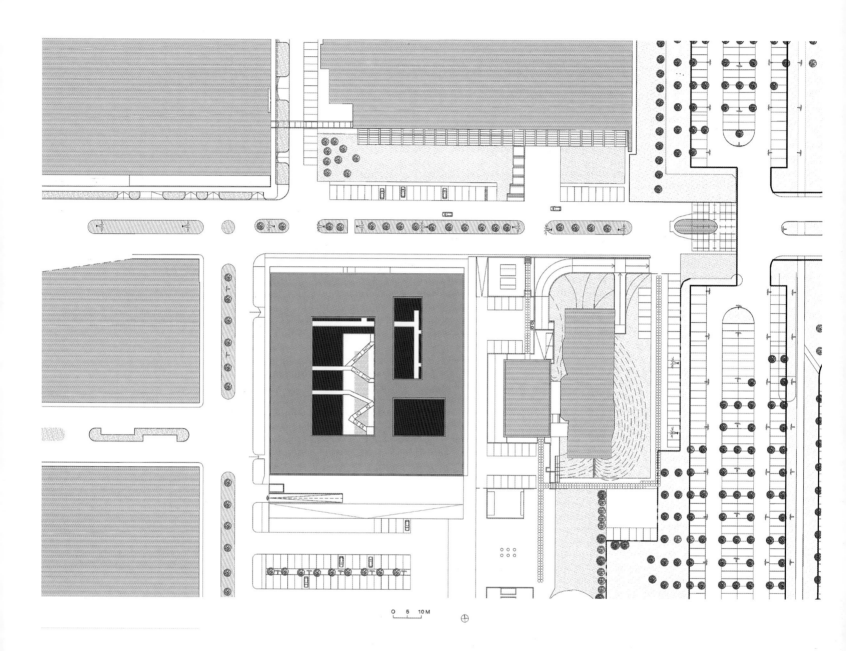

O   5   10 M

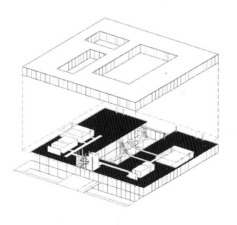

7. Detail of the east façade

8. View of the court

9. East façade

161

10. *Plan of the first floor*

11. *Plan of the second floor*

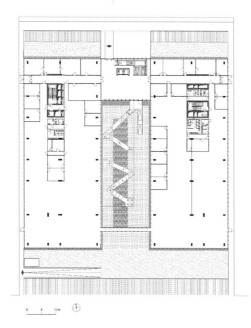

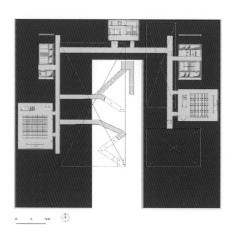

12. *Section*

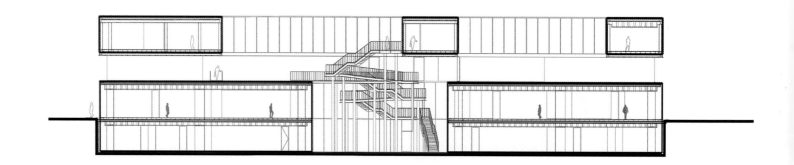

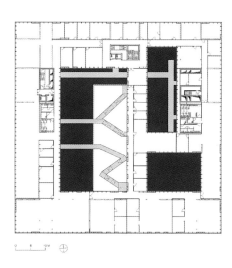

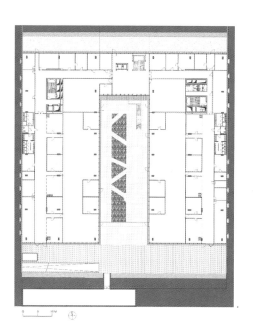

15. *Section*

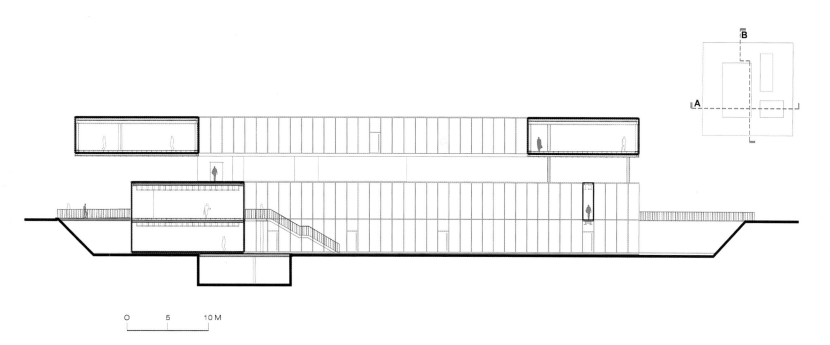

16. *Detail of the inner façade: relationship between the offices and the inner courtyards*

17. *Detail of the pools of water*
at the +7 m level

18. *The system of ramps and vertical ascents*
in the inner courtyards

19. *Detail of the glass walls opening onto the "red" meeting room*

20-21. *Detail of the interior and the air-conditioning system*

22. *Details of the spaces inside the offices*

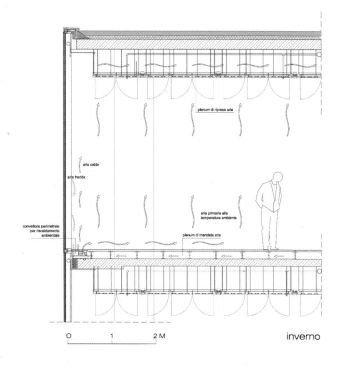

inverno

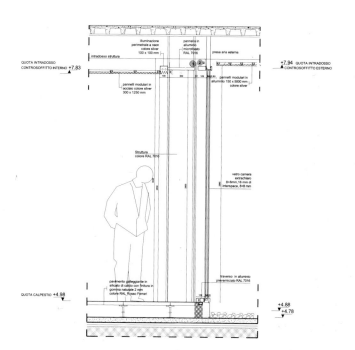

1-5. *Studio Azzurro. Megalopolis installations*

The 7th International Exhibition of Architecture at the Venice Biennale was inaugurated on 18 June 2000 under the direction of Massimiliano Fuksas. *Cities: Less Aesthetics More Ethics* was the title chosen for an exhibition that focused entirely on the complex social and urban context and on the responsibilities of the architect. A research that took up the legacy of reflections and discussions dating back to the sixties and revived the debate, involving professionals from the world of architecture, artists and intellectuals in the proposal of new utopias for the formulation of the "essence of architecture" in the new century.

Since 1999 an online expo and a competition had been attracting the attention and participation of new generations of architects, with the setting up of an open forum at the website

Ideas and projects to be presented during the event were available for months on the net, along with images transmitted live from different and distant situations in the citycams space, creating an urban tapestry. A picture of the city of the third millennium was built up from visions, suggestions and fragments through installations, models and videos distributed over a very large that extended from the Giardini di Castello to the Italian Pavilion and the Arsenale, Corderie, Artiglierie and Gaggiandre. Studio Azzurro was an integral part of the project and with the collaboration of RaiSat Arte made a video-itinerary presenting a panorama of places and remote cultures crossbred with the megalopolises and the new meeting places of humanity. At the Corderie a 7 x 5 m films of Hong Kong, Calcutta and Las Vegas along with airports, stations, shopping malls and decaying suburbs animated by people, faces and objects were projected by a total of thirty-nine projectors on to a 280-m-wide screen, accompanied by noises and sounds triggered by the passage of visitors. The route through the exhibition opened with the reception pavilion, a homage to universal peace, a scale model of Fuksas's Peres Center for Peace and ended, as the last stage in the exploration of the future of the city, at the Space Station nearing launch.

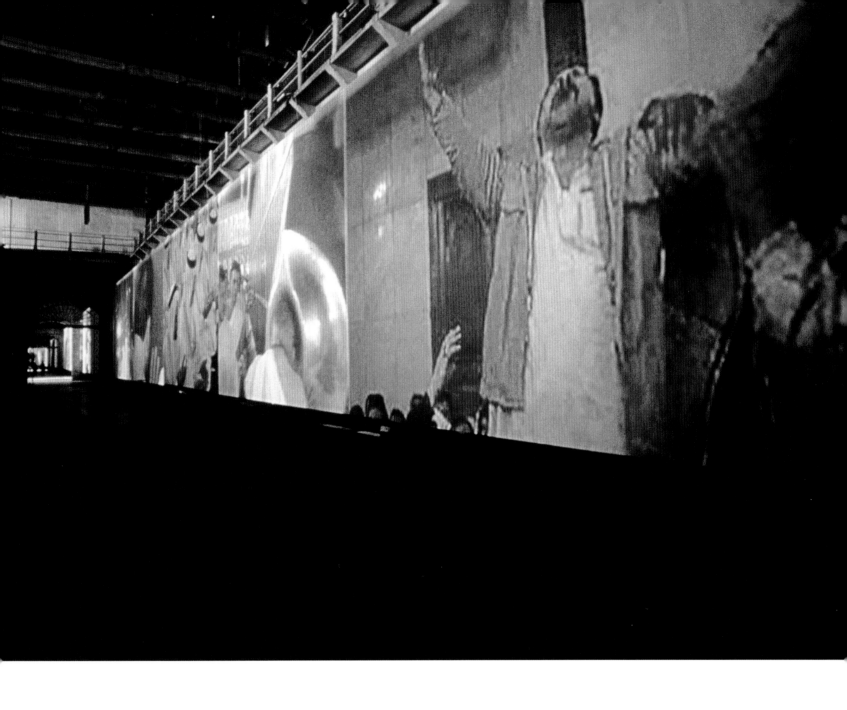

To inform about architecture

"The huge 280 metres by 5 videowall that we presented at the 7th Biennial of Architecture in Venice 2000, LESS AESTHETICS, MORE ETHICS, directed its attention at the megalopolis, seeking to find a scale of intervention that, after the utopias and the beginnings of the Modern Movement, no longer belongs to us. We recorded videos in eleven megalopolises [...]. We attempted to arouse an emotion, but above all to make people reflect"[1].

The impressive, very long sequence of images produced by Studio Azzurro and suspended in the void of the Corderie of the Venice Arsenal for the Biennial of Architecture in 2000, directed by Fuksas, fully demonstrated his complex philosophy of relations with images, the awareness of their emotional and political power, the magnification and complication of the various scales of relations between virtual and physical space.

The Biennial was an important moment of synthesis for an author who until that time had essentially only given a voice to his own works and heterogeneous actions in public projects, without ever having been able or willing to give a completed form to his reflections.

The appointing of Fuksas as director of the architecture sector of the Biennial made more than one academic and architecture critic turn their noses up; at that time, paradoxically, Fuksas was more well known abroad than in Italy and his image was more that of an eclectic and talented professional than of an intellectual capable of building synthetic and visionary images of contemporary architectural culture.

Yet from a certain standpoint, Fuksas was linked with the rediscovery of the radical inspiration of the previous Biennial directed by Hans Hollein[2], broadening its scale and increasing its echo to transform it into an operation that was both radical in its contents and choices and popular in its visual impact. For the first time the 2000 Biennial introduced authors and generations that were becoming definitively established on the national and international scene[3], but above all it imported to Venice unprecedented themes for reflection that attempted to push the delicate question of virtuality towards problems such as the contemporary megalopolis and the awareness and responsibility of the architect towards these new phenomena. The discipline was not tackled with the certainty of those who offer you solutions and slogans, but as an open problem requiring new words, open reflections, heterodox cultural and disciplinary interlacements. And the huge videowall, immediate in its choice and contents, expressed the desire to transform the Biennial into an increasingly broad-based, popular event, comprehensible to all without the need for explanations or introductory texts. Architecture had to return to speaking to people if it wanted to return to affecting everyday reality; architecture had to, and must still, resume listening to the new demands that a reality in continuous metamorphosis poses.

And the 2000 Biennial was tackled by Fuksas with an attitude of full awareness that the success of a cultural initiative passes through its popularity and ease of communication. An approach still looked upon with suspicion in Italy, but which enabled us to glimpse an ease of relations with the media and the practice of popular communication that Fuksas had acquired in France and that still remains today like a brand characterising many of the main authors of his generation.

The relationship with the media is by now a natural and structural element for the construction of the widespread popularity of a work, of its content and of the author himself; the relationship between marketing and architecture that is becoming increasingly complex and sophisticated with a view to a necessary global communication of the brand or one's own image, which sees architecture compete on the market on a world scale like any other communicable product.

And the promotion of the Biennial was through a very uninhibited and aggressive attitude in relation to the media, which enabled the edition to have more than 100,000 visitors in three months and to open a new season of Architecture Biennials that, even though they did their best to declare their extraneousness from – even hostility towards – the previous edition, inevitably had to follow the trail blazed in 2000 (in the 2002 edition, the new curator declared clearly that he would run an opposite Biennial in terms of content to the previous one, opting for an anthological approach in which the basic theme became, more than anything, a broad, comfortable frame rather than a real conceptual filter to look ahead and as a result the Biennial was transformed into an elegant but rather useless editorial updating action instead of an opportunity for reflection and action for the future).

But this Biennial, if referred back to Fuksas' direct experience, leads to a cross-eyed gaze at two themes that are distant from each other, yet linked conceptually: the architect's relationship with the media and advertising and the relationship with the use of images in project work.

In both cases the figure of the architect is presented with a theme that has traversed the whole of the 20th century and has grown progressively more sophisticated: that of the need to overcome the hiatus separating cultured and elitist modern architecture to become a popular, universally approved phenomenon. And if the first insight in this regard was by Le Corbusier, who used the language of popular advertising to communicate modern architecture, starting from the sixties this method slowly and inexorably transferred from the work to the author, from the object, from the language to be affirmed to

the name, which has become a logo, a trademark for the global market.

And the generation of Fuksas, Koolhaas, Nouvel not only fully acquired these contents of reality but interpreted them with great familiarity and boldness, knowingly mixing logo and message, market and contents, discipline and pop, and also representing one of the possible paths for the metamorphosis of our discipline in its relationship with the world. But the game is applied at two levels that touch each other ambiguously: the first, which sees the signature becoming a market logo (Koolhaas / Prada, Fuksas / Renault / the cloud logo / the Congress Centre in Rome)[4], the second, which uses popularity and above all its communication practices to convey new messages, more sophisticated and political contents with the conscious intention of provoking debate, of ideally turning niche ideas and actions into mass phenomena.

This was the case of the *Mutations* exhibition, directed for the Museum of Arc-en-Rêve in 1999 by Koolhaas, and of the following year and Fuksas' Biennial, when the centre of public reflection brought together a new metropolitan dimension and responsibilities of vision. So it was again, in Fuksas' case, with the recent polemic sparked over his participation in the inauguration of the new Fair in Milan, when a ceremony conceived just two days from the regional elections was considered politically inappropriate by the designer, who refused to take part in it[5].

The key point is that this news item immediately became an element of political polemic, capable of ending up on the front page of the most widely read national daily newspaper and of conditioning all the news and contents relating to the opening of the world's largest Fair exhibition.

So how could this gesture be interpreted? Astuteness, well considered political choice, news sense, a decision stemming from civil responsibility? Probably all these things combined, but with an important weight to be assigned to the author's awareness of his own social role and his capacity to entrust to the media messages that are easily generalisable. That is, that a large collective work of architecture is also an extraordinary communicative device[6], but it is also a civil, public work, also a gesture that intends to exaggerate the essential role that the architect plays as a creator, an active and essential player in the construction of quality within the new metropolitan landscape.

With this polemic, Fuksas takes to a maximum tension a typically modern mechanism that links on one hand the signature as object, but on the other plays actively with the very contemporary awareness of architecture as a communicative medium, as a work knowingly filled with contents in which gesture becomes logo and vice versa, also producing the risk of an excessive levelling of the content of complexity and richness that an architecture can express.

A risk present above all in the emulators of this practice of architecture-marketing that, if it is not combined with experience and talent and above all if it is not confronted with architecture as a discipline, may dangerously transform itself into a simple, fatuous advertising action that sees the architect more as a decorator than as a creator of complexity in which to live.

"You need only move back to read three façades simultaneously, realising an urban effect: simultaneity of vision.
Did you want to create a cinematographic effect?
Yes.
Does cinema condition your works?
Almost all of them.
Which cinema?
The cinema that architects like: *Blade Runner,*

Brazil, but also all the cinema of Wim Wenders, of Altman. I was particularly struck by *1989 Escape from New York* and *Back to the Future*, one of the early Spielberg films, which magnificently simulates the end of architecture. There architecture becomes a conceptual place"[7].

"Many of my projects represent passage, the desire to pass from one idea to another, to then pass from the moment of conception to the realisation. For Europark in Salzburg, as in other projects, my reference was a film, *Point Break* by Kathryn Bigelow, which tells the story of a group of surfers. The strongly characterised roof houses the car park and at the same time is the sign of reference; it is a wave, a homage to liberty. [...] In effect, my dream was to see people walk on the roof"[8].

The intense relationship that Fuksas maintains with cinema as a product of the imagination populated with images born and consumed in everyday reality opens up an interesting window not only onto the complex relationship between images as resource and insight into the project, but also onto the work of architecture conceived as a talking, communicative element. Together all this is shaped and worked through a relationship with the media and digital technology, sophisticated and elementary at the same time.

Since the late nineties Fuksas has used digital technology as a resource to multiply ad infinitum insights into space and form that till then had been economically unaffordable and visually rather impractical. Digital helps Fuksas give concrete form to an insight of his already formulated in 1986 as an interpretation of "architecture as an effort of the image to lose form", but it also boosts the construction of a vision to help dream, multiplying the ambiguous relationship between image of reality and its realisation. A policy of the image that is dangerous for those who do not know how to control it, that tackles the competition action realistically as a sophisticated practice of immediate advertising and also architecture as a machine generating images and also emotions.

When for the entrance to the caves in Niaux (1988-1993) Fuksas created a monumental design, brutal and immediate, advertising design and also a hint at the images of a primordial reality that we are to meet; he clearly gets to grips with the view that the gesture, as well as making architecture, becomes its story and logo.

A few years later, with the Europark in Salzburg, Fuksas creates – necessarily, it being a large shopping centre – an architecture as a communicative system with a large red roof, but above all with the façade / sign whose night-time image is reflected in the moat of water surrounding it.

In recent years, with these works, as with others executed in parallel by Koolhaas, Hadid, Herzog & de Meuron, we witness the completion of the process that sees a work and its success on the basis of quality of its spaces, but above all of the capacity they have as logos to puncture the screen, establishing themselves in global communication.

But the great fortune that architecture has had with respect to other media is its necessary, final concreteness, which sees the image ultimately renounce the quality, or not, of the spaces that it has attempted to sell or to represent. A *proof of the pudding* that makes more than one architect's blood run cold and that also becomes another element of narrative, of expectation from the public prepared by the expectation of the meeting with the real space.

Thus it was for the new Fair in Milan, with a success with the public that will increase over the coming years, as it is now for the Congress Building in Rome, the true challenge that awaits Fuksas for the next three years.

But the continuous relationship with cinema also expresses well the desire to conceive the lived space as a place of continuous, contradictory, individual and fragmented experiences of life that encounter the sequences of designed locations as with a story that must interest and seduce continually and that must also have the force and structure to change with a reality in profound and constant metamorphosis.

[1] M. Fuksas, *Frames*, Actar International, Barcelona 2001, p. 243.
[2] The 6th Biennial of Architecture, Venice, 1996, "Architetto come sismografo" and the exhibition staged within it and directed by Gianni Pettena "Radicals. Architecture and Design 1960-1975".
[3] We need only think, among other things, of Gary Chang, Lacaton & Vassal, Metapolis, R&Sie, Francesco Jodice and Armin Linke, Didier Fiuza Faustino, Stalker, A12, Greg Lynn, Kas Oosterhuis.
[4] See: S. Casciani, *Pubblicità e architettura*, but above all the sequence of frames taken from the ad filmed by Fuksas, in M., Fuksas, op. *cit.*, pp. 180-195.
[5] P. Conti, *Fuksas: voto vicino, non inauguro la Fiera con Berlusconi*, in "Corriere della Sera", Thursday 24 March 2005, pp. 1, 10; reply by the President of the Lombardy Regional Authority, Roberto Formigoni, again in "Corriere della Sera" pp. 1, 12; to then find in all the national newspapers the polemical reply by PM Silvio Berlusconi to Fuksas, issued during the inauguration of the Fair on 1 April.
[6] In 1990 Fuksas gave a lecture in Paris entitled "Architecture et publicité" in which he clearly stated the necessary and positive role of advertising for the work of architecture and the need to reflect on a media potential not yet explored.
[7] M. Pisani, *Fuksas architetto*, Gangemi Editore, Rome 1988, pp. 67, 68.
[8] M. Fuksas, op. *cit.*, p. 55.

Postage stamp commemorating the opening
of the New Rho-Pro Trade-Fair Centre,
April 2005

**Nardini Exhibition Centre and Auditorium, Bassano del Grappa
(Vicenza, Italy)**

1. *Study sketches*

2. *The auditorium and the "bubbles"*

The "bubbles" were created as part of an extension of the establishment of the historic Bortolo Nardini distillery at Bassano del Grappa. The initiative stems from the desire of the current proprietor of the firm, Giuseppe Nardini, to use contemporary architecture to renew its image on the occasion of the anniversary of 225 years of existence.

The complex is inserted right next to the old building, in a park designed in 1981 by Pietro Porcinai, one of the most interesting Italian landscape architects of the 20th century. The client's request was for the construction of a research centre with laboratories, offices and a multimedia facility, along with a conference hall able to cope with the hundreds of people who come to visit the distillery every day. Massimiliano Fuksas received the

commission and decided to design an original work that would at the same time be respectful of the tradition and history that permeate the site and the brand created in 1779. The decision not to touch the parkland and trees became fundamental for the architect, who chose to protect them with a thin mesh, making them untouchable and calibrating his own action in the space that they enclose. Out of the same requirement came the decision to locate the 100-seat auditorium underground, with access by means of a gentle descent. The flight of steps is framed between two walls of bare concrete, covered with a lawn that can be used as an open-air auditorium when necessary.

The offices are housed in two elliptical and slightly staggered blocks of glass that seem to float in the air. The bubbles, whose shape

is inspired by those of stills and bottles of aqua vitae, are at the same time a futuristic form that plays with the curved line, the light and the reflections. They appear to barely rest on the sloping piles that are in fact suspended from them, with the weight borne by the central steel structure of the lift.

The bubbles are entered by ramps, spanning the pools of water underneath that are used in the daytime as skylights for the conference hall and at night as sources of light. The upper one is designed to serve as a multifunctional space and the lower one houses the laboratory. Their outer surface has a green colouring that accentuates the reflections and blends into the garden while, on the inside, the completely transparent glass offers a clear view of Montegrappa.

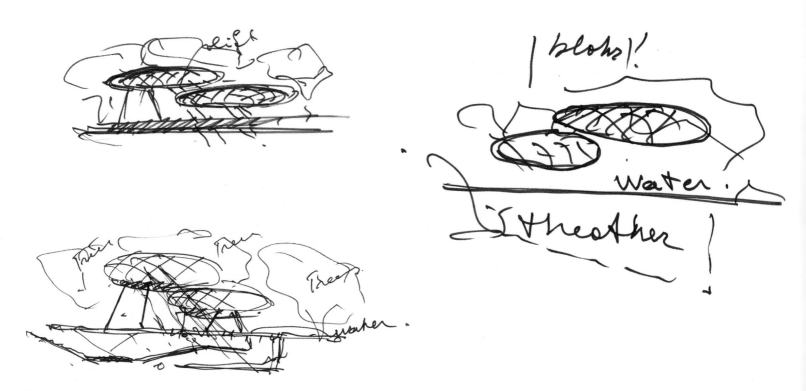

3. *Section*

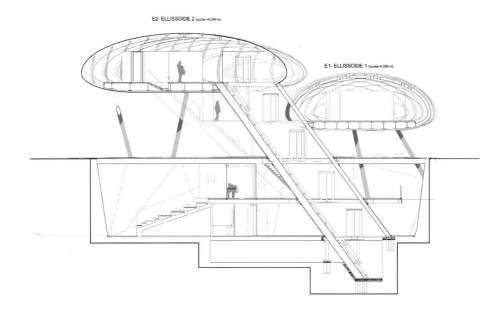

E2- ELLISSOIDE 2 (quota +6.246 m)

E1- ELLISSOIDE 1 (quota+3.096 m)

4. *Plan, height 3.10 m*

5. *Ground floor plan*

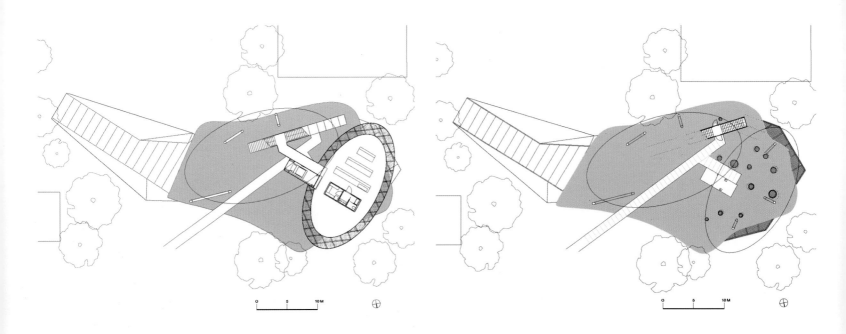

0   5   10 M

0   5   10 M

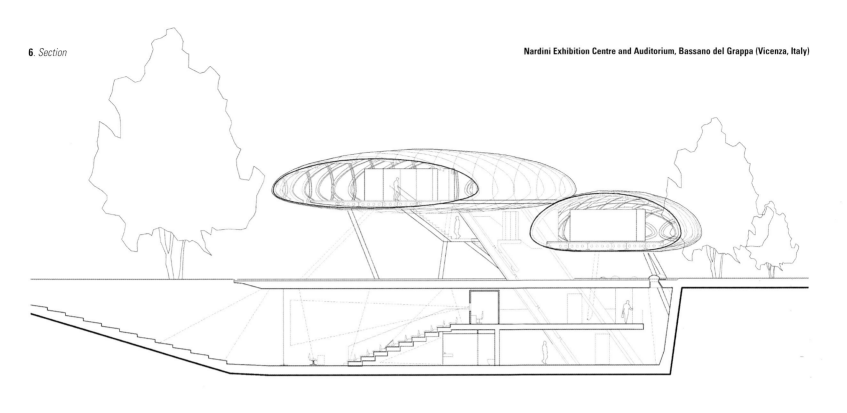

7. *Plan of the auditorium*

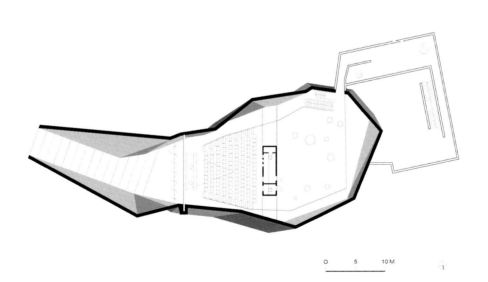

O   5   10 M

8. *The bubbles in relationship to the pool of water and the "Porcinai" garden*

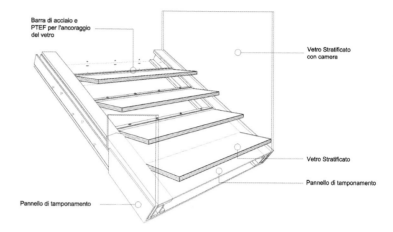

Barra di acciaio e PTEF per l'ancoraggio del vetro

Vetro Stratificato con camera

Vetro Stratificato

Pannello di tamponamento

Pannello di tamponamento

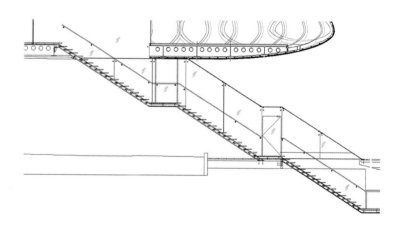

14. *The connection between the two "bubbles"*

15. *View of the inside of a bubble; on the right the steel box of the toilets*

16. *Structural detail, centring*

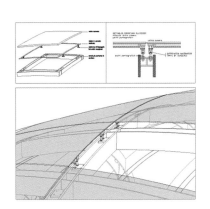

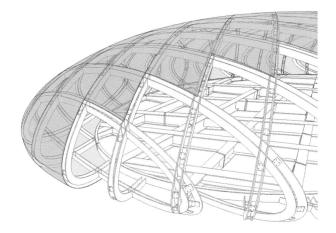

17. *View from the inside, detail of the centring
and the bubble structure*

18. *Sections and plan, height 3.10 m*

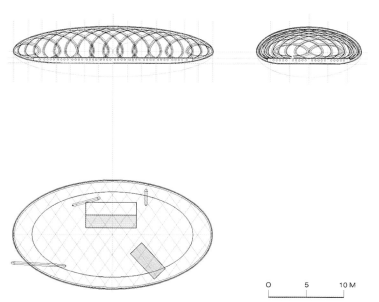

O   5   10 M

19. *Detail of the bubble from inside*

20. *Prospect of structures*

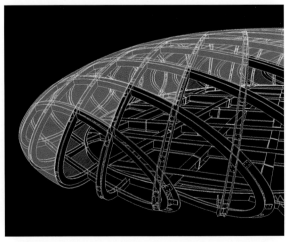

22. *Detail of the toilets for the auditorium;
on the wall a video-installation by Filippo
Macelloni*

23. *View of the underground space
at the entrance to the auditorium*

Conversation with Giuseppe Nardini, Bassano del Grappa, April 2005

The Nardini "bubbles" provide an exemplary case of a client who is enlightened and attentive to the value of quality in architecture, above all thinking of the contemporary Italian situation.

How did this adventure come about? What needs and what demands have guided the choices made?

Giuseppe Nardini: In 2001 we had recognised the need to build, near to our plant, a structure in its own right, autonomous, inserted into the existing context and to be used on one hand as a space for meetings and on the other as a laboratory.

In recent years food and wine tourism has developed a great deal, with an ever more interested and growing public, and the spaces we had available were not sufficient and above all did not have a clear identity. We also wanted a space to use for cultural events and small exhibitions.

So we discussed this for a long time within my family, with my children, Cristina - who has followed this initiative a great deal -, Antonio, Angelo and Leonardo, to understand above all how to create this new space.

2005 is the 225th anniversary of the Nardini company, so we decided to give ourselves a present, to promote a major work of contemporary architecture to celebrate our anniversary and also as a gift to the town of Bassano del Grappa.

Since unfortunately there is little contemporary architecture in Italy and we have scattered ugly goods sheds and works of low quality all over Veneto, we thought it was the duty of an entrepreneur to favour a cultural operation of scope to generate a major work of artistic architecture, without this meaning we would fail to meet our own specific needs.

In this specific case, the task was simplified by the fact that we wanted a particular structure with less binding functional requirements, but that was above all a symbol for the Nardini of the near future.

How did you arrive at Massimiliano Fuksas?

Nardini: Once we had decided what to do, we began to look around. I love contemporary architecture and I had seen the latest things created in Veneto by Renzo Piano and Mario Botta; but we wanted a work that testified to the sense of a break with the past, with a strong innovative drive. If possible, we wanted an Italian author and also someone known abroad, so we gradually arrived at Fuksas.

How was the meeting and the relationship with Massimiliano Fuksas?

Nardini: A major reciprocal enthusiasm was immediately created. Fuksas very much liked the idea that a family company had embraced such an ambitious cultural ideal.

And a feeling came about that has enabled us to work well together.

But did you set limitations for his intervention?

Nardini: We immediately defined a very limited zone for the project; furthermore, the intervention, with its structure above ground, had not to be obtrusive in the panorama, the surrounding territory, and above all was not to touch the trees planted following a garden designed by Porcinai in 1980 as a complement to the factory.

Most of the space was supposed to go below ground, with the auditorium for conferences and public events, but without the intervention being transformed into a bunker.

And what was your reaction to the initial proposals?

Nardini: We were immediately very surprised and enthusiastic.

The idea of the two bubbles came about on the morning of our first meeting on site; at the end of lunch, at the restaurant Fuksas asked for a white plate and drew the two bubbles. And what I liked as time went on was that Fuksas has remained faithful to his early formulation. This experience enabled me to understand that Fuksas is first and foremost a painter, an author, who has a decisive vision for the identity of the project, which he is then to develop and reinforce cohesively over time, but without ever abandoning it.

Fuksas supervises the worksite from a distance, as do all great architects; but in his projects the cohesion of the project is absolute, maintaining a fixed vision.

But the greatest satisfaction came with the final result, which exceeded all expectations. I still remember a precise moment, with the work finished, us two alone in front of the *bubbles*, staring in silence at this architecture. I remember I felt a strong emotion; I looked at Fuksas and I had the clear sensation that we were sharing the same emotion, one in which reality outdoes the vision and wins for its unexpected strength.

Then the work interacts well with the insertion among the trees, also on account of how they are covered with those large nets…

Nardini: You see, the net had been put up to protect plants and also to prevent the leaves falling onto the water during treatment, then we noticed that the nets worked very well with the bubbles, so we kept them!

I would also like to say that, in contrast with other works of architecture that prefer a particular view, this is a work that is beautiful from all angles, because the space lends itself a great deal and we strongly desired this effect.

All the trees have been respected to the millimetre, with their foliage, and also for love of the work of a great Italian landscapist.

I was struck by the fact that one of the conditions applied in the realisation of the work was that craftsmen and firms from a radius of within 50 km of the plant were used…

Nardini: With this choice we wanted to confirm something of which I am firmly convinced, namely that we still have excellent companies and craftsmen in our area.

And the constructed work has been a happy confirmation of this fact.

In practice, where possible, we have worked with plant installers and with many craftsmen who know how to do anything, plus we had the good fortune to have leading companies near us, such as Sunglasses, crucial for the glass windows and walls, whose technicians were present on site almost every day.

Other problems that emerged on site, such as the mechanisation of the windows, were resolved in situ, but the craftsmen were also involved for the construction of floors, roofing, the lights and the choice of these, the steel coverings; in short, most of the details, except a few elements.

I believe it is very important to support the widespread richness of talent that exists locally. For instance, in the last few days some craftsmen specialising in the construction of machines for the production of gold chains have been making the robot that will clean the outside of the bubbles.

The small worksite enabled control and work that was almost hand crafted, with the logic of each-day-as-it-comes and the possibility of motivating the craftsmen and workmen involved a great deal.

What do you feel every time you encounter the space and what reactions have you noticed in the visitors?
Nardini: Many people, above all those with a greater sensibility, talk to me of emotions; this is a work that offers emotions and that is the most beautiful thing that architecture can produce.

And how was it welcomed in the territory, since this work can be seen as a useful provocation and also a work of excellence?

Nardini: I have noted that the public administration has grasped the importance of investing resources and attention; it is something necessary and important for the future.

What can we ask of Italian architecture today?

Nardini: I see that still today we make new developments around our historic centres, with constructions that cannot be considered architecture, because they are worse than those built in the post-war period; there is speculation without any quality, without attention to the landscape and the environment, yet where major resources are earmarked without any consideration. It would be enough if certain civil and industrial buildings were at least decent; if people want to intervene, they can, they only need to want to. It is a pity because we no longer respect the environment; Veneto, which was stupendous, has become so ugly in recent decades.

And this, unfortunately, is the result of the economic boom, of excessive wealth, without this being accompanied by education about the quality of the landscape and our resources.

24. *Entrance to the auditorium*

Competition for a stadium, Salzburg (Austria)

The project is located in an area into which the city has recently expanded, used chiefly for the construction of large-scale facilities for which it is necessary to provide new spaces for the development of infrastructures capable of withstanding the environmental impact of their insertion and the flows of traffic to which they give rise. The client for the work is the SWS Wals-Siezenheim of Salzburg, which held a competition for the city's new stadium that was won by the Fuksas Studio. The proposal it came up with entailed the study of a system capable of dealing with the question of the specific features of the territory and allowing the creation of an organism able to adapt autonomously to the context in which it is set. The solution has been drawn up on the basis of the presupposition that the architectural choices should not be conditioned by the location but be independent in the planning phase from the pre-existing natural and artificial elements. The idea found concrete form in a structure that incorporates the sports ground and advances into the surrounding area, extending its presence within it. The effect is obtained by the realization of a membrane supported by a framework of pillars and steel girders of irregular shape that envelops the reinforced-concrete structure of the terraces and continues on one side to create a reception area. The configuration assumed by the object rejects any reference imposed by the landscape and any symmetry dictated by the central ring.

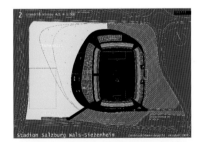

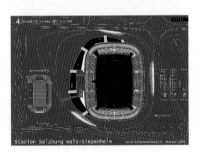

1. *Plan basement floor*

2. *Ground floor plan*

3. *General layout plan*

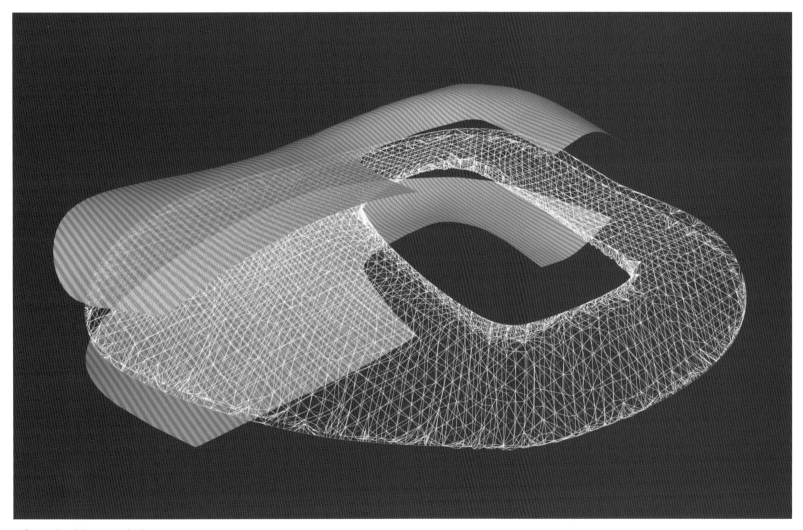

4. *Perspective of the structural scheme*
of the stadium roof

5. *Sections*

6. *Structural details of the roofing*

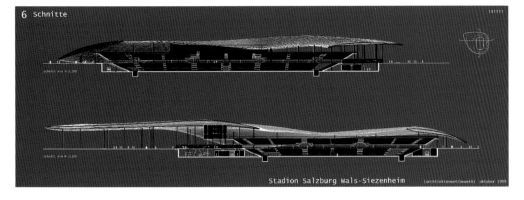

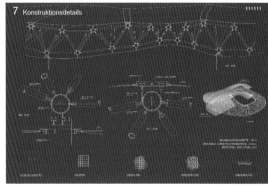

Competition for Berna Hall, Brünnen (Switzerland)

The area of intervention is situated at Brünnen, a holiday resort not far from Bern, next to the motorway. The shopping mall called for in the competition held by the Migros Group is located in a residential district created under the Nutzungszonen und Bauklassenplan, which has regulated the expansion of the city in this area. The structure devised by Massimiliano Fuksas creates a system of pedestrian and vehicular connections with the houses, utilizing main axes and routes intended for public parkland. The park, located to the east, is set between the old people's home and the Garten-center and is a fundamental part of the project, which blends in to the west with the protected area of forest. The link with the belt of new constructions is further consolidated by a significant landmark formed by the concrete-and-glass roof of the mall. The roof is designed with an enveloping form that spans the motorway, modifying the degree of transparency of the material to favour the identification of the sports facilities present. Its upper configuration changes along the route, revealing successively the wall for free climbing, the Mediaplex, the hotel, the chute of the swimming pool and the garden centre of the Baumarkt.

The Funsc@pe, a name embracing the concepts of amusement, information and landscape, combines leisure activities, cultural initiatives, spaces for shopping and landscape in a single container, serving as a point of reference for the emerging community.

The complex also comprises a hotel and an old people's home; the former, facing west towards the forest and housing 119 suites, forms Brünnen Square together with the Mediaplex and the conference zone and is conveniently connected with the Fitness Centre and swimming pool; the latter, consisting of two blocks stretching into the area of parkland, is located next to the station.

The system is designed to present a continually changing appearance and offer observers thousands of different views as they pass through it. Its objective is not to crystallize in any particular form but to leave the final conformation forever open. This mechanism introduces a gene of change into the organism that will make possible any future expansion.

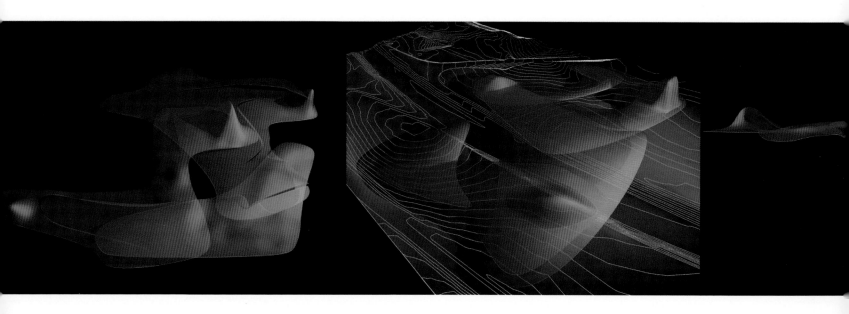

1-5. *Digital simulations of the roofing and the spaces as new artificial landscapes*

6. *Detail of the section of the central gallery*

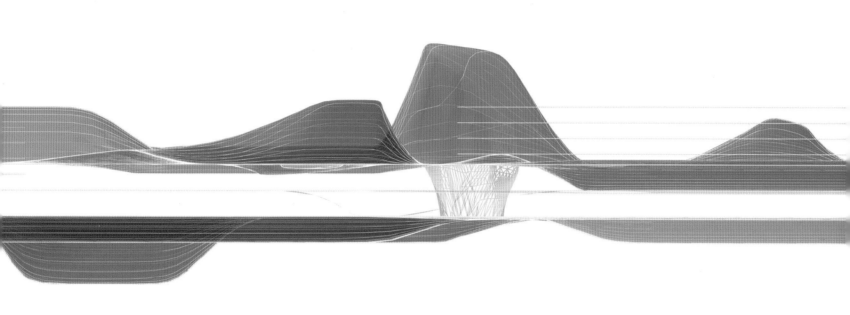

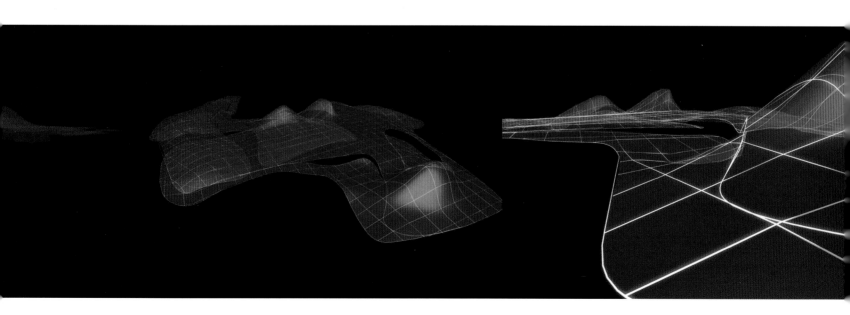

7. *Section of the main roof, model*

8. *General view*

9. *Digital simulation of the roofing of the complex*

10. *The central section of the gallery*

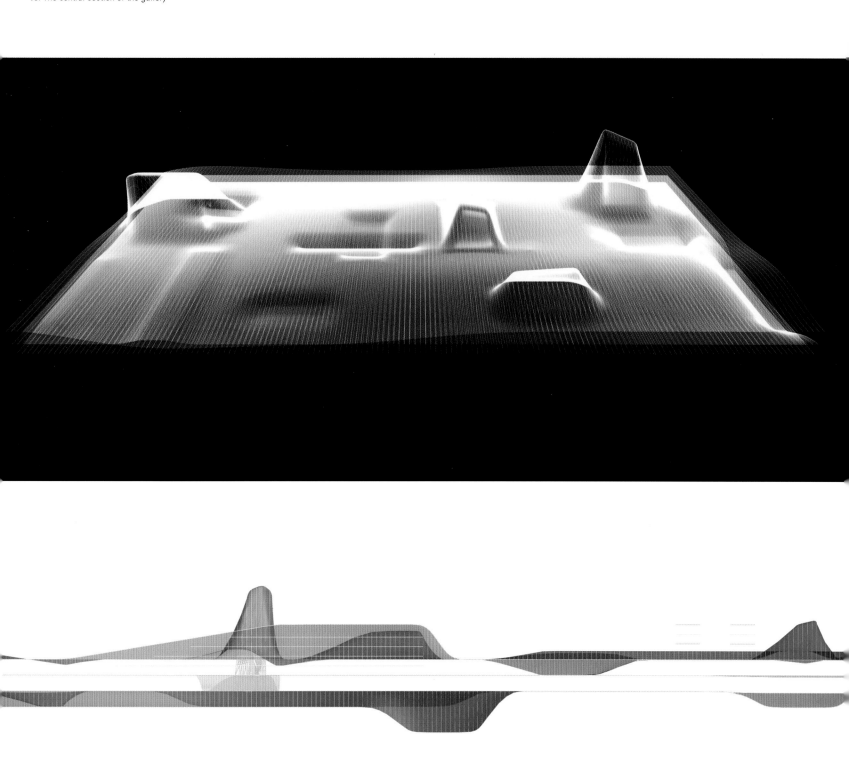

New Trade Fair, Rho-Pero (Milan, Italy)

1. *Detail of the offices in relationship to the roof of the central gallery*

The new trade fair is located on the site of the former AGIP refinery at Rho-Pero, an area of over 2 million m² that has recently been reclaimed, and close to functional infrastructures of urban and territorial communication that it is planned to develop further.

The complex was commissioned from Massimiliano Fuksas by the Fondazione Fiera Milano following an international competition by invitation staged to provide the city with a larger trade-fair district situated outside the centre.

Conceived as one of the largest exhibition venues in Europe, covering an area of around 465,000 m², the structure will also be an attractive place for meeting and exchange. It will comprise eight pavilions, two of them on two levels, a building with four towers to be used as a Service Business Centre, 80 conference rooms, 45 bars, restaurants and stores laid out

in an area of about 9500 m² and offices and support services with a total area of 6500 m².

The gigantic system extends for 1 km and 300 m along a central axis serving a series of symmetrical sheds, characterized by a large undulating roof of steel and glass. At some points the "Vela" exceeds 30 m in height, forming "craters", "waves", "dunes" and "hills", and is supported by metal columns with a diameter of half a meter that split into six branches, permitting enormous overhangs.

Light and transparent, it shelters and transforms the space that it traverses, defining the continuity of view along a linear expanse already prepared for future growth. The axis embraces the backdrop of the Alps, following a public pedestrian route that runs from east to west at a height of 6.50 m.

The structural conception in reticular glass

and steel utilized for the "Vela" is proposed again in the "Logo", a 36-m-high dome resembling an ocean wave that covers the large hall and conference room of the Service Centre. A common feature of the two incisive architectural signs is the complete absence of standardization of the components, which are unique in their shape and size, numbered and not interchangeable.

The whole project for the new Milan Trade Fair is inspired by the need to impose order on the route between the various sectors, creating a fabric of architecture, nature and life in which the glass-and-steel structures, arranged in a line, reflect and duplicate the trees, water and visitors. At the same time the Trade Fair is conceived as an "open" fragment of the future metropolitan structure that will spread out from Milan to embrace, over the course of time, the whole of the north-west area as far as Malpensa.

2. *Perspective of the central gallery, competition project, 2002*

3. *General view of the glazed central gallery; in the background, Milan*

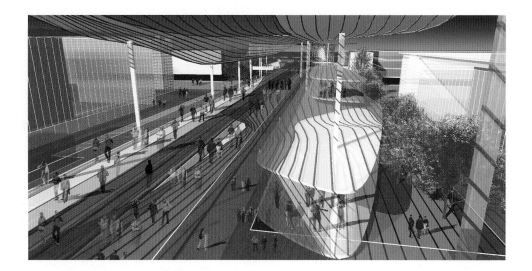

4. *General layout plan*

5. *Aerial view of the new Trade Fair*

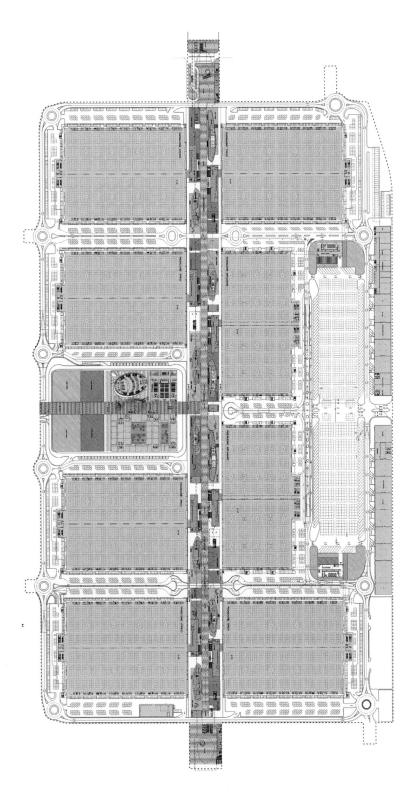

209

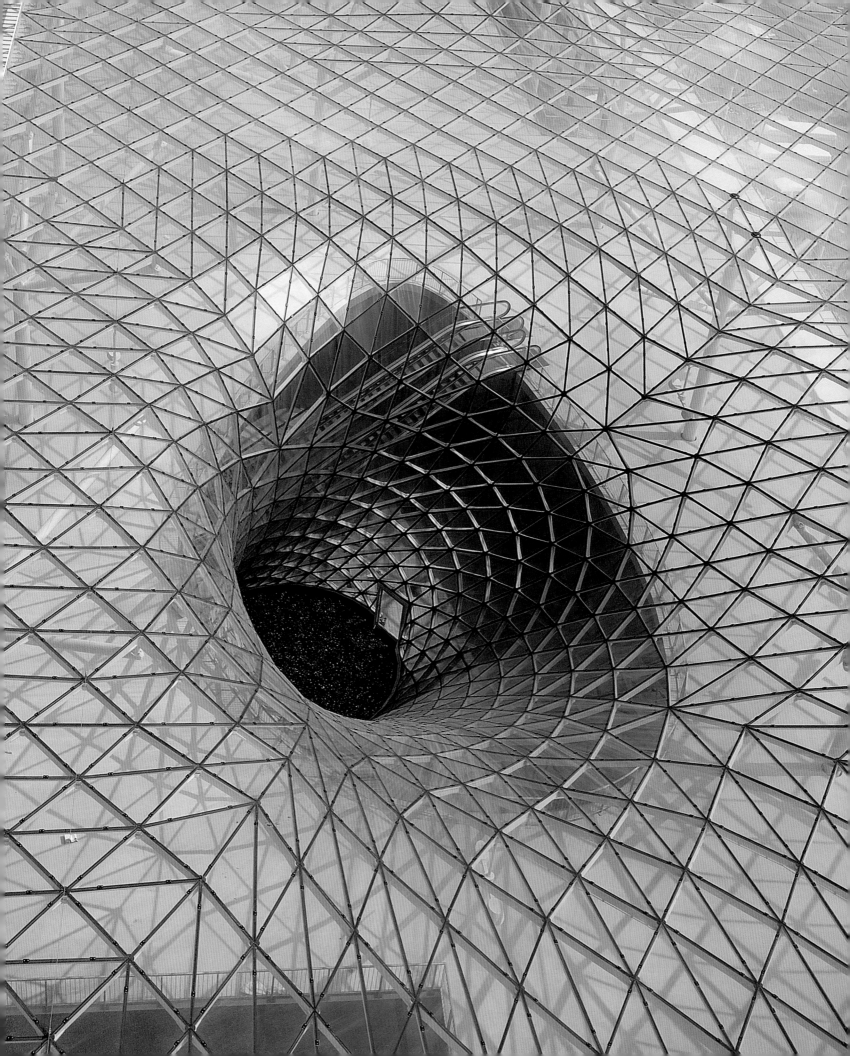

9-12. *Structural details of the pillar and roof of the central gallery*

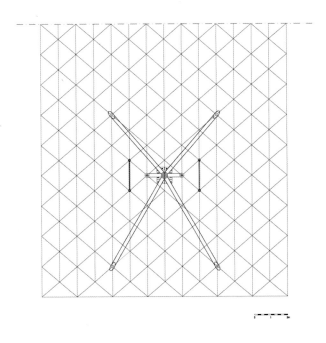

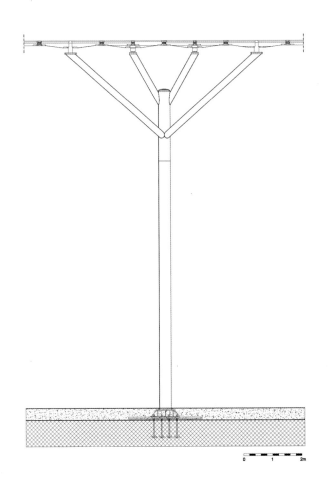

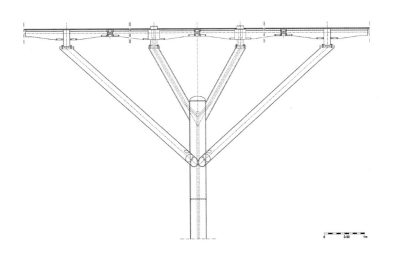

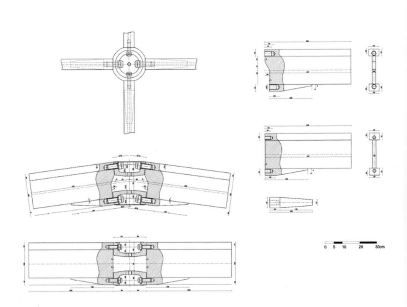

15. *Elevation type B*

16. *Longitudinal section of type B*

17. *South elevation of the reception*

18. *Cross section type B*

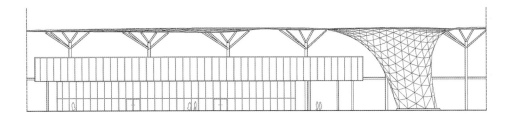

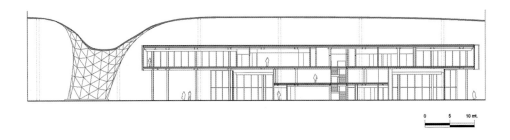

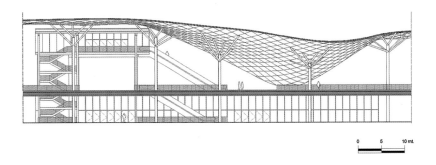

24-25. *The offices and the central gallery*

26. *Plan of the offices*

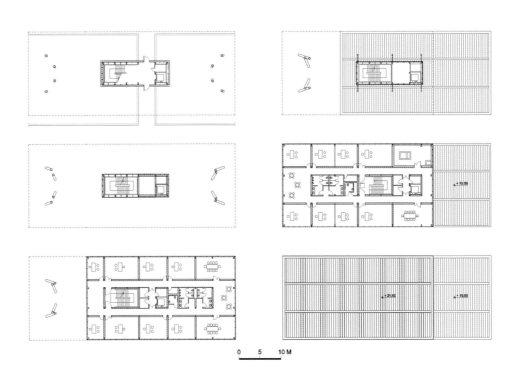

0   5   10 M

27-28. *The type B pavilion in relationship to the central gallery and pavilions of the Trade Fair*

29. *Plan of type B, height 6.50 m*

30. *Section detail*

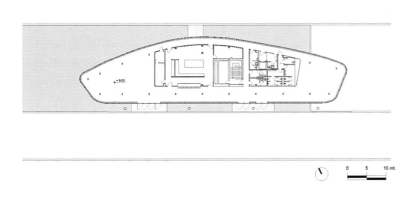

0 5 10 mt.

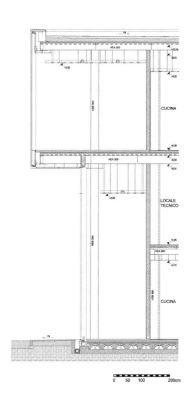

39. *View of the lateral pavilion*

40. *View of the pavilion under construction and the skylights*

41. *Construction detail of the skylights*

42. *The exhibition pavilions and lateral pools*

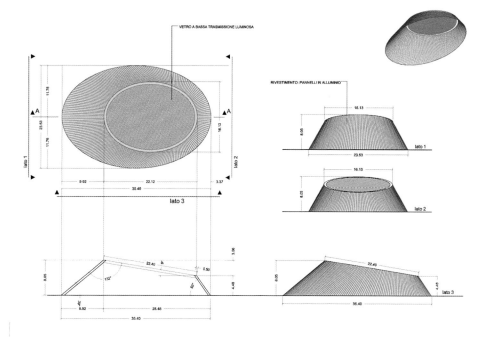

43. *The entrance to the auditorium*

44. *General view of the roofs; on the left,*
the cone of the auditorium

45. *Plan of the auditorium at height of 6.50 m*

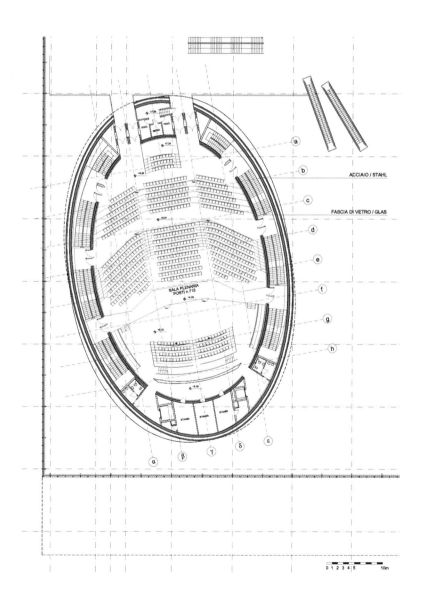

ACCIAIO / STAHL

FASCIA DI VETRO / GLAS

46. *Detail of the roof of the cone of the auditorium*

47. The entrance hall of the auditorium

48. The auditorium in relationship
to the office area and the main entrance

Conference centre, Frankfurt am Main (Germany)

1. *Virtual model of the central roof*

2. *Perspective, view from the street*

The intervention for the Frankfurt MAB Zeil is located in Frankfurt, on a site of 105,000 m^2, just a few meters from the banking district along the Zeil, an important commercial street from which it takes its name. The zone was previously occupied by the city's main post office and the headquarters of Deutsche Telecom, as well as a series of buildings that have all been demolished, including Frankfurt's first skyscraper, the T-Hochhaus, built in 1954. The lots covered by the project centre on two different catalyzing poles, the Zeil and the historic Palais, which will be reconstructed in exchange for the municipality's offer to increase the maximum building height to 100 m. Thus the whole of the planned urban development formalizes a drastic change in the scale of the surrounding architectural fabric, hitherto dominated by constructions of small and medium size. In this zone, in fact, will be built the towers designed by

KSP Engel & Zimmermann Architects and the multifunctional complex of the Fuksas Studio, winner of the competition held by the MAB Zeil Forum GmbH & Co in 2002. Fuksas has designed a futuristic entertainment system that comprises a shopping centre, cinema, fitness centre, hotel, halls for events, offices and car parks, covering a total area of about 70,000 m^2. A fluid form, called on to control the uninterrupted flows of users coming in and going out at different times, with personal directions and requirements. A completely glazed building, in which the various activities are subdivided with respect to the two large, original nuclei, which steer users toward two types of offer, linked respectively to an atmosphere of relaxation or a formal space.
The solution lies in the structure that has been devised, organized on several levels with different entrances, including one which leads from the front directly to the

fourth floor, where the cinema, sports centre and restaurants are located.
Underneath is set the independent shopping centre, illuminated by a system of large voids traversed by a sequence of escalators and lifts that run the full height of the building all the way down to the shops on the ground floor, accessible from the street as well.
The hall of the hotel is reconstructed inside the Thurn & Taxis, close to the art gallery, offices and more elegant shops. The rooms are located on the upper floors, while the intermediate levels house the conference centre and sports facilities.
The translucent skin envelops and deforms the whole construction, turning it into a single transparent volume. Through its façade, the MAB Zeil communicates the variety of functions to be found in the same structure, drawing the life of the city inside and becoming part of it.

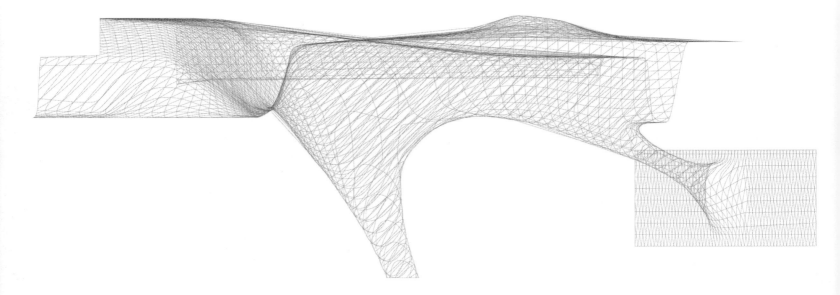

3. *Plans*

4. *Sections*

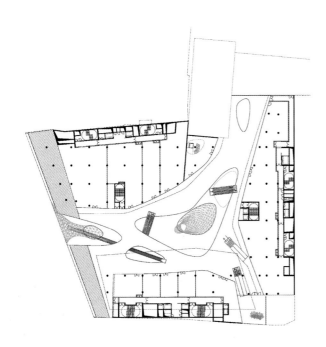

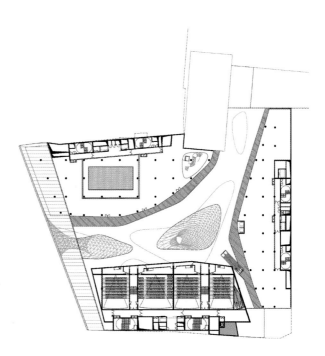

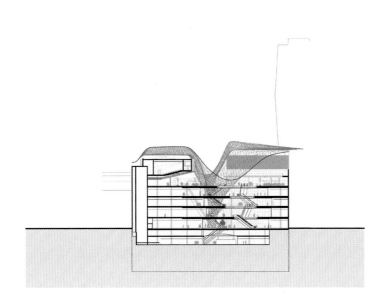

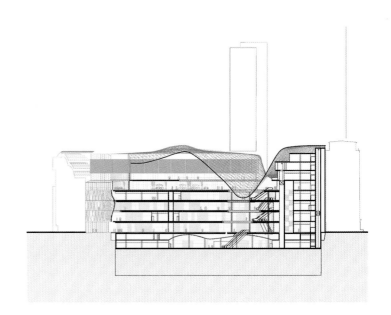

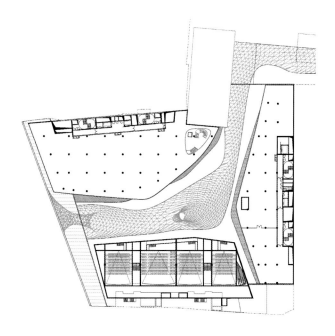

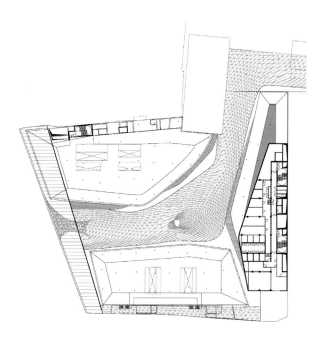

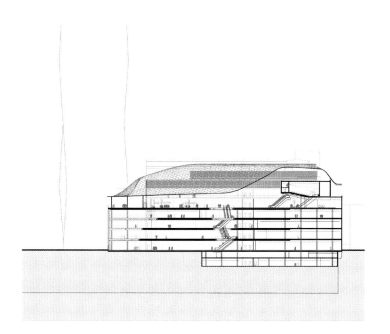

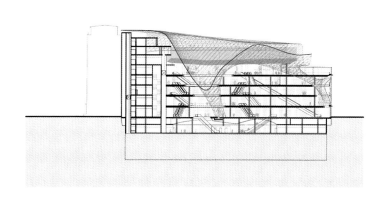

5. *Prospect, view of the main façade*

6. *Prospect*

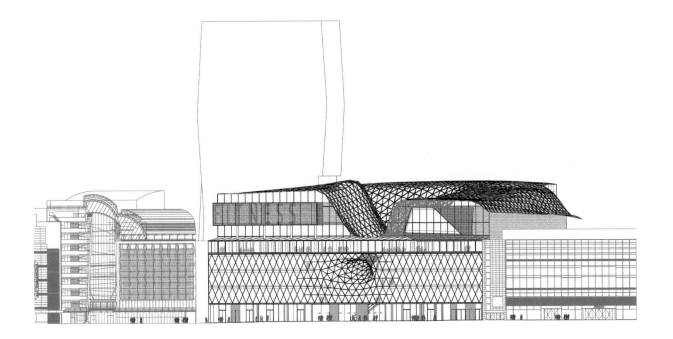

7. Prospect, view from the street

New concept for Armani, Hong Kong (China), Shanghai (China), Milan (Italy)

The projects for showrooms in Hong Kong, Shanghai and Milan constitute the latest skilful effort on the part of the Armani label to expand its market, by creating new sales outlets that aim to cover a broader commercial range. A decision that has been taken with the intention of redefining its image through a sophisticated synthesis of fashion and architecture that brings to bear the extraordinary injection of creativity produced by the encounter between different identities.

The prestigious label, linked for the Giorgio Armani Boutique to the architect Claudio Silvestrin, has entrusted the design of the Emporio Armani sector to Massimiliano and Doriana Fuksas, partly to guarantee a successful combination of personalities inspired by different approaches to design. The aim of going beyond the idea of a simple shop to create an alluring meeting place is shared by the three sales points, which are located in highly commercialized contexts, presenting themselves as interventions capable of giving a new identity to existing spaces.

The multi-store in Hong Kong is set, in fact, in a tower already under construction. Laid out on three levels with a total area of 3000 m^2, it has large windows opening onto the urban landscape of Chater Road, in the heart of the Central District. The space in Shanghai, around 1100 m^2 in area, is located on the

ground floor of a historic building dating from 1912, the Three on the Bund, former seat of the Union Bank, on the eastern edge of the British concession granted in 1846. The Armani Jeans shop in Milan has been opened in a particularly significant location, Corso di Porta Ticinese, former entrance to the city and now one of its trendier districts.

In addition to the Emporio, the former comprises a flower shop, a bookshop, a cosmetics shop and a restaurant, outlined entirely by a strip of red-lacquered fibreglass measuring 105 x 70 cm and 8 m high that, wrapping around itself, is transformed from a bar counter into an independent entrance. The clothing display area is marked out by two walls of curved, engraved and illuminated glass that present garments and accessories in a setting that tends to change with every variation in the light.

Its intensity alters during the day, reflected off the floor of bright blue epoxy resin that, creating an effect similar to water, multiplies the dimensions in all directions thanks to the ceiling of the same colour that breaks down every visual barrier.

A fluidity refined and accentuated through every detail and through the doubling of the planes, attained by mixing up the elements, makes it possible to accompany the movement of customers and motivates the transformation of the settings. The result is an architecture that calls attention to every

shift in perspective, to every change, and that tends to create an effect of immateriality by deliberately deflecting every visual impression.

In Shanghai the same aim is achieved through a design in which sinuous routes and neutral walls are multiplied, expanding the space *ad infinitum* by means of a cunning choice of materials. In the diffuse light, perception is cadenced solely by modulating opacity and transparency, directing the gaze from the back-lit walls to the ceiling and floor in resin. Everything has a white coating, imparting a sense of unity to the setting and making the red furnishing accessories, the cylindrical cubicles for trying on clothes and the objects on display stand out. The Armani creations are attached to a curved bar that runs right through the space and, illuminated by luminous pipes, marks out the entire route. A similar solution is used for the lighting system in the Milanese jeans shop, where incandescent tubes of plexiglass of different lengths hang in a cascade from the ceiling, creating a studied play of light. Here too the result is that of a theatrical setting in which the red and blue of zones devoted to shopping and rest areas alternate, reunified by double-panelled wooden walls covered by a double layer of PVC that, bending between shop and lounge-bar, help to present the dimension of the event.

1. **Hong Kong**
Axonometry, entrance and restaurant

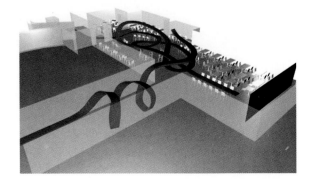

3. **Hong Kong**
Plan of the restaurant

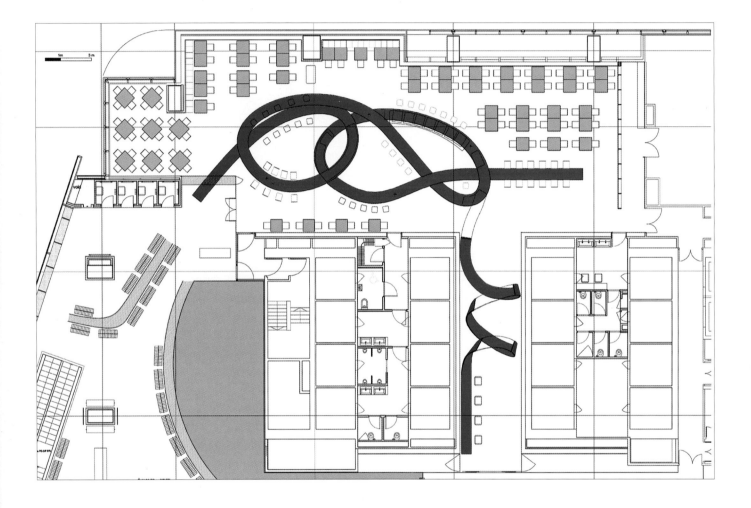

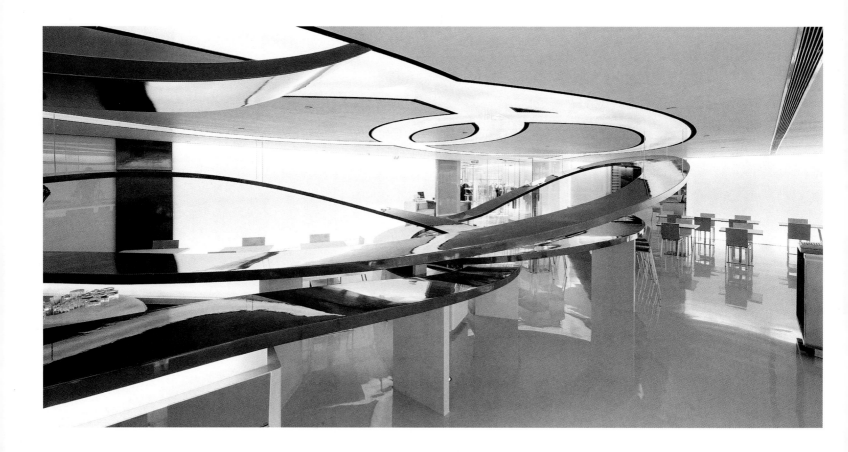

7-8. Shangai
Views of the showroom

9. Milan
View of the bar

10. Milan
Detail of the staircase

Conversation with Giorgio Armani, Milan, April 2005

The Armani store in Hong Kong represents an interesting evolution compared with the structures previously created for fashion. It is no longer just a shop, but a centre in which the various market sectors have their own specific spatial identity and in which the visitors' experiences and emotions are placed at the centre of attention. What has changed with Hong Kong? And what does Hong Kong represent in the evolution of Armani stores?

Giorgio Armani: The Emporium Armani in Charter House, in Hong Kong, is part of an even more complex project that develops over three floors and that, for the first and perhaps only time, presents two premier lines in the same building: Giorgio Armani and Emporium Armani. Because in one of the most prestigious areas in Hong Kong, the Central District, a complex of offices and shopping centres of great value had been realised, designed and built by Hong Kong Land, the leading city group in investments, the management and development of the real estate sector, and it had seemed appropriate to us to concentrate the new store there. Armani Charter House is located in the heart of the Central District, and every day tens of thousands of people pass through it, making it an incomparable venue for presenting the Armani universe under a single roof. The characteristics of the Emporium, in fact, take on a particular prominence if compared with the Giorgio Armani boutique: 750 square metres on the ground floor, protected by an imposing pale stone façade, never interrupted by windows, appearing as a symbolic icon of what the shop houses. Where stone characterises the Giorgio Armani boutique (designed by Claudio Silvestrin), glass and light are the essential elements of the Emporium; it is a futuristic environment, an open interactive space where people can meet up and make purchases, taking up and extending that tendency towards friendly interaction that I had already expressed in the Milan store in Via Manzoni. In Hong Kong too there are the areas of Armani Cosmetics, Armani Books and Armani Flowers, which I find is one of the most spellbinding: a long corridor of opacified glass along which a slate slab stands out, giving you the feeling of being in a greenhouse. Yet it is a fluid, uninterrupted space, which enables any object to be contained; its leitmotif is a beam of red light, almost a ribbon that winds quickly and concentrates gazes on itself.

How did you arrive at Fuksas? What had struck you about his previous work?

Armani: I feel a curiosity about and a great attraction to architecture, which I consider the true art of the 21st century. It is a passion that has grown over time and has prompted me to collaborate with various architects, from Michael Gabellini to Tadao Ando. As regards the work of Fuksas, he was introduced to me by my colleagues, who had prepared a complete portfolio taking account of some of my requirements: capacity for innovation, freshness of vision, great experience but not in fashion. Those who design a boutique for the first time can contribute an originality, an innovation that others do not have. At that time I was looking for inventions in form, language and materials: Fuksas' works, his projects for the Aerospaziale agency in Rome and for the EUR congress centre, had the fluidity, the lightness, that I wanted. I very much liked the mall designed for the Europark in Salzburg and its concept of shopping centres as new plazas.

What dialogue is established between client and designer and what initial requirements had been formulated? Has the initial concept changed very much over time, and if so, following whose suggestions?

Armani: We talked a great deal: the dialogue with Massimiliano and Doriana Fuksas was the most important piece in the project mosaic. I wanted the Emporium Armani in Hong Kong to address the public in a different way, brighter and more open, where everything has a precise style, decidedly Armani, but organised with variations, modelled according to the sectors. It was a unique, unrepeatable project, which was to have a particular style, and so it was, evaluating together, detail by detail.

What particular dialogue did you attempt to build up between the store and context that welcomed it? As well as having a different structure and different lines, do the two projects for Hong Kong and Milan also have their own particular identity, arising from the place where they are located?

Armani: Of course places and constructions influence each other. In Milan the Emporium Armani was created inside a period building, designed by architect Enrico A. Griffini in 1937 for Assicurazioni Generali, so with the symbols of the cities of reference – Venice, Trieste, Milan – and with statues representing Life, Time and Providence. It is a historical building, which expresses a precise style and history and which had rigid planning restrictions, such as the internal corridor developed like a road, to be respected. Armani/Charter House, on the other hand, has been designed from the exterior, integrating Armani's personality with that of the city and its raised pedestrian walkways.

What were the inputs and the philosophy behind the new store in Milan for the youth line?

Armani: The characteristics and objectives of Armani Jeans are different and particular compared to the Emporium Armani. And my requirements were different too: to design a repeatable concept, one that would also maintain its characteristics in different concepts, characterising them in a youthful, dynamic way, but without any point in common with what are called "jeanserie" – jeans shops –, which are characterised by a large quantity of goods displayed in total confusion. So the walls have been lightened and protected by a PVC cloth for industrial use, concealing the defects and highlighting the merits, just as you do with an item of clothing around the body, while the garments have been hung from a tube running across the middle of the room along the ceiling. I also consider the materials very interesting: bright or resined stainless steel, transparent Plexiglas, small mirrors of polished steel to direct the lights. It is an experimental concept, reinforced by a design that makes no reference to classical geometry. Inside I also wanted an Armani Jeans Café, organising its various offers as the day passes, from croissants in the morning to tasty aperitifs for the evening. Because I like to think that shopping can become an experience, multiplying sensations and opportunities to meet.

What was Giorgio Armani's experience inside the Hong Kong space the first time you visited it finished? And what would you like the visitor entering this highly fascinating space to feel?

Armani: I am notoriously not an easy man to satisfy, and working with me is a daily exercise in discipline and control. But the results are there, and when I entered the Emporium in Hong Kong for the first time, I experienced a sense of gratification and satisfaction, above all seeing its quality and elegance, superior to those of the city's other multistores. I hope this is also the impression aroused in visitors, mixed with the pleasure of a warm and hospitable welcome.

As a client who continues to invest in new spaces for commerce and meeting, what does Giorgio Armani expect from contemporary architecture and what role do you think it must have today?

Armani: I think architecture is art and communication at the same time. That it can express a complex and representative system of values. That it illustrates its time, but also a tension towards the future. I also think that private clients, with their requirements, contribute to articulating a language that is reflected on the territory where the intervention of architects – I am thinking about the large urban developments and the new districts – is subject to profit and loss accounts that are too reductive. With the results that we continue to see: horrible built-up areas in the motherland of design.

1. *General layout plan*

2. *Plan*

3. *Prospect, general view*

4. *Longitudinal section*

The new Zenith space will be built in the municipality of Eckbolsheim, on the A 351 Autoroute, at the west entrance to the city of Strasbourg. Its location has been chosen by the city of Strasbourg, client of the project through the Société d'Aménagement et d'Équipement de la Région de Strasbourg, in a suburban area that has undergone considerable development. The future infrastructure will contribute to the formation of a new urban hub that has been planned to improve the present seat of the European Parliament. The lot assigned to it measures about 14,000 m^2 and is located in the larger area set aside for the large Exhibition Park.

The competition was won by Massimiliano Fuksas in 2003 and fits into the series of public works he has carried out, commencing with the Zenith in Paris in 1984 and continuing with the one in Amiens. In fact the architect received the commission to design a hall for performances and concerts capable of holding 10,000 spectators.

The building, intended to serve as a magnet for international attention, aims above all to attract an audience of young people. A new construction, an incisive architectural landmark, able to stand out from the flat urban fabric in which will be set. Its image is characterized and made recognizable from a distance by a bright orange colouring that is also used inside the hall. A membrane of fabric covers the elliptical form imparted by the steel skeleton, tautening along the curves and, illuminated from the inside, permitting a dynamic play of light. The sensation of continual transformation that this produces is augmented by the projection of the calendar of events on the outer surface.

The entrance is set in the glass wall situated in the steel base and leads to the hall. The foyer, 5 m high, is surmounted by a ring of polycarbonate and permits the transferred form of the ambulatory to be taken in at a glance. The interior, built of reinforced concrete, is organized around the stage located in a central position and covered by a dome of curved steel.

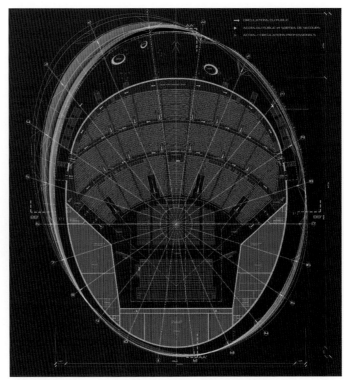

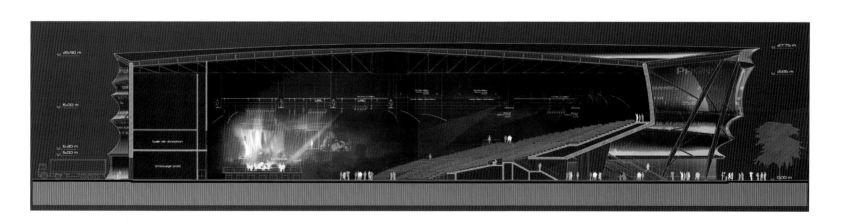

Exhibition centre, Astana (Kazakhstan)

The project is located in Astana, seat of government of the young and vast republic of Kazakhstan, one of the wealthiest countries in the region. The operation forms part of a broader plan of definition of the new state, implemented after 1990, the year it obtained its independence. An initiative born out of the need to create a pole of territorial reference with a recognizable identity that starts out from the basic objective of choosing a city of emblematic location and characteristics and shaping its image as capital. It is in this perspective that the IAA (International Academy of Architecture), an association engaged in the development of initiatives linked to the diffusion of architectural research at a worldwide level, was asked by President Nursultan Nazarbayev to make a

contribution to the development of a national culture. The cooperation between public and private bodies found its first concrete expression in the staging of an international competition by invitation for a theatre and exhibition centre for the city, to be used to redesign an area of around 30,000 m^2.

The Fuksas Studio took part along with five other architectural studios, and presented a design for the exhibition hall. The proposed complex is made up of a series of volumes of different sizes all organized around a main building. The different functions prescribed by the programme are located in several pavilions, differing in their dimensions and form but with the common matrix of a truncated cone. At the centre stands the

building of the theatre, a large cylinder stretching out towards the entrance and dominating the wide avenue at whose end it is set. The general layout consists of curvilinear blocks placed on linear routes, marking out its visual directrix. The representative route of approach to the concert hall is flanked on both sides by pools of water bounded on the outside by rows of tall trees that can be reached by short footbridges located at the level of the ponds. All the buildings are designed to be clad in steel on the upper part and panes of glass on the lower one. Thus the system is apparently suspended in mid-air and the effect is amplified on the curved surfaces by the reflections created by the light, multiplied infinitely by the continual movement of the water.

1. *Prospect, general view*

2. *Prospect, view from the water*

3. *Model*

4. *Model, study of tensions*

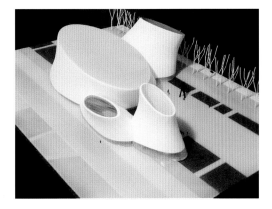

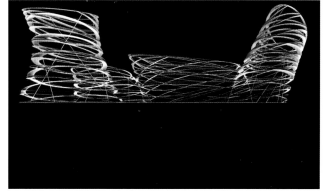

De Cecco Management Centre, Pescara (Italy)

The Fater S.p.A business district will be located in a degraded area of Pescara, devoid of any particular architectural or environmental features but with interesting possibilities of development provided for by the current town-planning scheme. In fact a considerable expansion of the road system is expected, giving the whole area, characterized by a diffuse urbanization, a strategic role in the communications between the north-west and south-east parts of the city. The new building will stand next to the future road axis known as the "Pendolo" on a lot situated between Via Salaria Vecchia, Via A. Volta and the Strada Comunale Piana, taking the place of a series of recently demolished industrial sheds. The structure commissioned by De Cecco sets out to be self-sufficient from the functional viewpoint and to create a

pleasant working environment, equipped with all the necessary services and designed to be capable of modification over time to meet the company's changing requirements. Standing out from the adjacent constructions because of its scale, the complex is made up of two superimposed blocks: an L-shaped one that is 21.34 m high and has an area of 9070 m^2, on which stands another, ring-shaped volume with a height of 24,66 m and an area of 4118.05 m^2. The first, more linear block is articulated by thin floor slabs and deep empty spaces that allow light to penetrate; the form of the second, with a strongly contrasting reticular structural façade, makes it a dominant feature in the surrounding fabric.

The managerial sector is concentrated in the ring, while the offices and support areas are located on the first two levels. These include

the hall, connected visually with the library and learning centre through a two-storey-high circular hole, along with meeting rooms and communal spaces. A continuous skin of glass facilitates the total freedom of organization of the rooms inside and their constant permeability.

A marked gap between the two blocks creates a wide terrace that serves as a comfortable meeting place with a panoramic view. Both are linked vertically by a common system of connection but have different arrangements of their horizontal routes, parallel to the sides in the lower part and radial in the upper one. It is possible to walk in the open around the whole perimeter of the building, which maintains a constant relationship with the outside and the nearby sea, on a path that has sections surfaced with natural materials like gravel and wood.

1. *Model, detail of the wall covering*

2. *Model, view from above*

 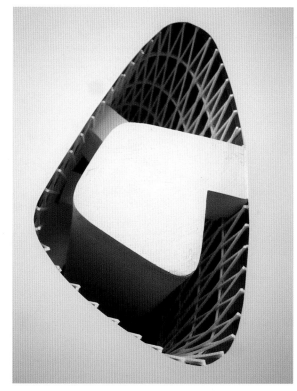

3. *Model, general view*

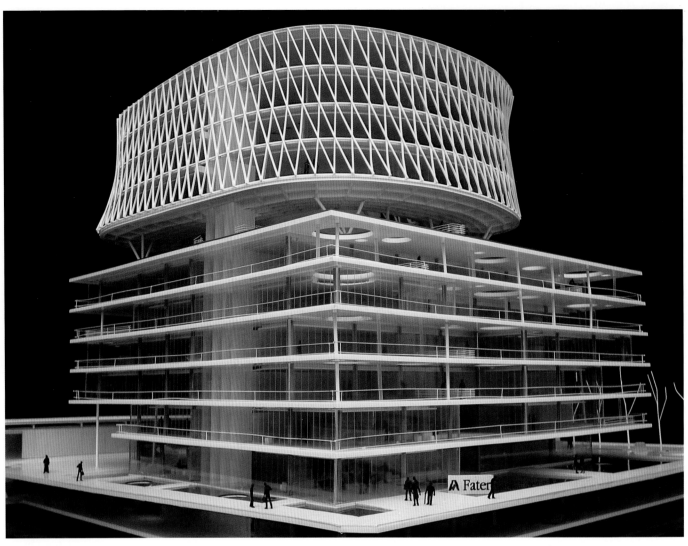

4. *Model, general view*

5. *Plan of the eighth floor*

6. *Plan of the third floor*

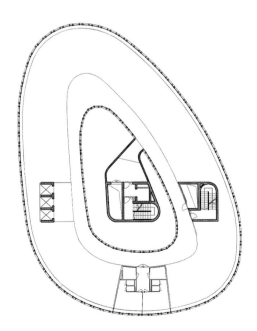

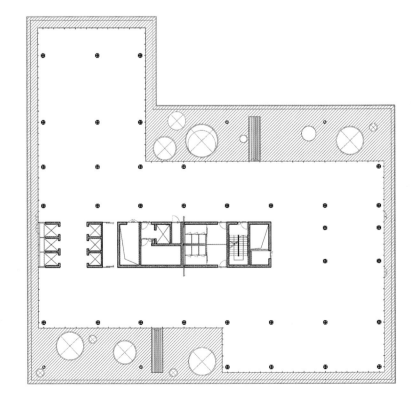

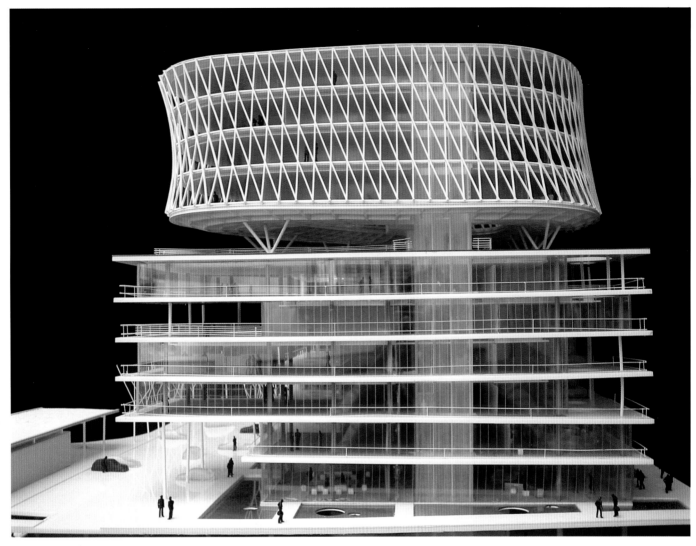

7. *Model, side view*

8. *Section*

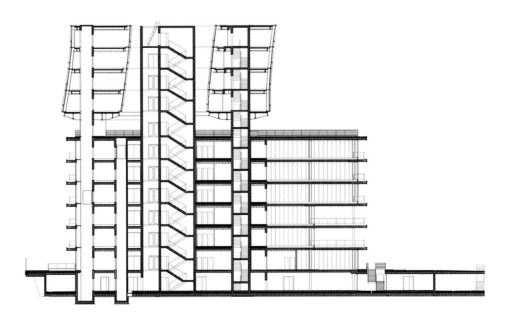

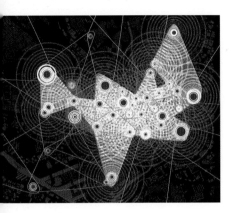

The intervention is located in Salford, a borough to the south-west of the great conurbation of Manchester. The area, situated close to the entrance to the city, represents one of the most valid opportunities for the economic revival of North-west England. The intention of the Central Salford Urban Regeneration Company is to revitalize the borough from the bottom up and create new jobs over the space of twenty years that will trigger a dynamic cycle of public and private investment in the area. The competition for the upgrading of the area, held in 2004, was won by Massimiliano Fuksas in partnership with the Canadian Joe Berridge. The proposal of the two architects focuses on the creation of a strong identity capable of imparting unity to a badly disjointed fabric. The operation entails re-establishing a close connection between their existing districts and routes, along the north-south axis, and linking them to the larger urban centre on which the whole area depends.

The programme envisages a development of the road network, already underway, to regulate the traffic entering and leaving from and for Manchester, a reclamation of the free spaces left between the constructions that would make the most of their different potentialities and a formal and functional improvement of the land along the Irwell River.

The rediscovery of a liveability becomes the objective pursued by the plan, which aims at the introduction of a closer relationship between the inhabitants and the site. The consolidated arteries of communication, such as Chapel Street and the M602, are transformed into tree-lined avenues while the abandoned railway lines become green corridors equipped with cycle paths and roller-skating tracks.

The image of the area is redrawn by new structures for entertainment and leisure, green spaces and illuminated routes. The large viaduct sheds its condition of "urban void" to be adapted on several levels as a container of multiple activities, and a new residential area takes the place of the industrial zone along the Irwell, offering a valid housing alternative for the community. The informing concept of the project accompanies all the choices, aimed at turning the imposed barriers and limits into points of junction and links that establish a new relationship with water and nature, in which it is possible to recognize the specific individuality of the place and the product to be exported.

1. *The strategic relations between the different centres and public spaces*

2. *General perspective*

3-4. *Digital simulations of the new spaces and public containers*

Stazione Duomo is on the Piazza Dante-Centro Direzionale section of Linea 1 of the underground railway in Naples, in the sector that corresponds on the surface to the junction between the straight stretch of Corso Umberto I, the connection with the railway and the axis of Via Duomo.

The project is part of the programme for upgrading the city's underground transport system, aimed at turning places of transit into opportunities for travellers to come into contact with contemporary art and architecture. One of the great names invited to produce these works was Massimiliano Fuksas, to whom the Metropolitana di Napoli S.p.A. entrusted the design of the station in Piazza Nicola Amore.

The initial idea put forward by the architect has undergone various modifications in the course of its execution, following the discovery of a temple dating from the I century AD, a Hellenistic colonnade from the Flavian era and a race track belonging to the gymnasium. The altered circumstances have had a considerable influence on the conceptual handling of the whole intervention, which has assumed the interaction between archaeological park and underground station as its basic theme.

In the new proposal the finds, brought to the level of the underground railway, are made part of the design. The route starts from the square, where the skylights in the form of a truncated cone, simplifying the organization of the accesses, signal the existence of the intervention below ground to the city. The descent to the tracks is transformed into a journey through the incomplete excavations which evokes the excitement of the discovery. People are carried down by escalators, which control the time taken to reach the depths. Arriving underground, they are gradually exposed to the view of a central awning that protects the archaeological finds, separating the streams of passengers from the places where visitors can stop. Set against the bulkheads along the route, four "fragments" of sprayed concrete, finished with epoxy resin, punctuate the perception of the system all the way to the platforms next to the tracks.

The display of finds in showcase-portholes set in the walls is accompanied by videos projected on plasma screens and free-standing pieces of columns. The setting is permeated by a warm light produced by numerous sodium floodlights sunk in the floor and ceiling in apparently haphazard fashion. The diffuse light from the three skylights in the form of a truncated cone, on the other hand, illuminates the temple and the tracks, avowed protagonists of this atypical archaeological park.

1. *Model, view of the interior*

2. *Model, view of the entrance*

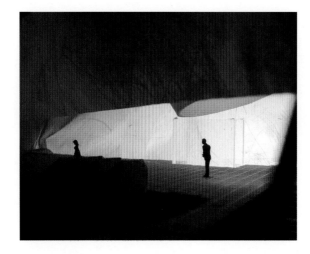

3. *Prospect, view of the interior*

4. *Section*

5. *Plan, actual state*

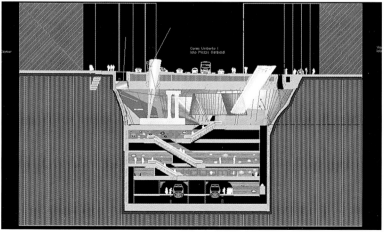

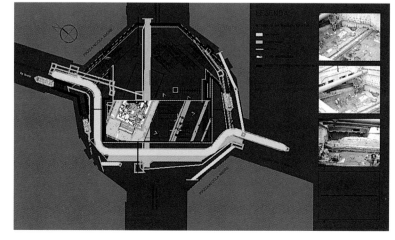

Competition, London (Great Britain)

The Olympic Aquatic Centre is one of the structures that the British Department of Culture, Media and Sport plans to build for the Olympics of 2012. It is one of the most significant projects in the bid to win the games, owing to its position right at the entrance to the Olympic park and the role that it could play in the future development of the Lower Lea Valley, where it is located. The intention is, in fact, to provide the games with a fully equipped Olympic swimming pool that can subsequently be turned into a centre of excellence for water sports. The operation would allow the town of Stratford to attract a considerable number of new tourists, reviving its economy.

The proposal submitted by Massimiliano Fuksas is a functional and symbolic system, a strong signal that will not lose its representative and visual attributes with the cutbacks that will be necessary following the prestigious event. The building, in the hypothesis presented, provides a visual link between the city, the valley and the stadium and serves as a landmark identifiable from every side, a point of reference for the whole area that will also attract attention outside it.

The scheme envisages an intervention in four sectors, to be allocated respectively to the Aquatic Centre Building, the bridge, the temporary constructions for the Water Polo Venue and the support areas.

The main structure is an organic form with an ovoid plan, moulded like a sculpture and without a privileged front. The configuration assumed makes allusions to the sea, like a shell protecting what it embraces, but never appears gratuitous as it is modelled by the spaces designed to house the various activities required by the programme. The outer surface is clad in steel and translucent material that is sensitive to changes in the weather and season, presenting an appearance that alters continually with modifications in the light. The roof is supported by three feet set on the ground that separate the entrance area from the main swimming pool, maintaining a constant fluidity between inside and outside. Under it is set the podium, comprising the swimming pools and related facilities, with one zone above the ground floor in which all the functions public are located and another below it housing all the official functions, the athletes and the media.

The centre is designed to hold 20,000 spectators in the stands, some of which will be permanent while others are conceived as protrusions of the basic form. Modular and easy to assemble, these are covered like inflatable balloons with a special fabric stretched over steel frames. At the end of the Olympics, the temporary tiers of seating will be turned into green areas and replaced in a reversible way by the new façade of the sports centre.

1. *Study models*

2. *Model, general view*

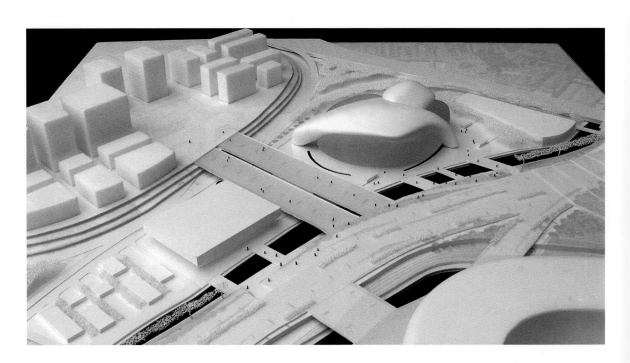

3. Generale prospect

4. Model, view from above

5. *Prospect, view from the inside*

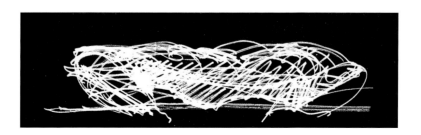

Centre des Archives Nationales de Pierrefitte-sur-Seine et Saint-Denis (France)

The new national archives of France will be built at Pierrefitte-sur-Seine et Saint-Denis, a locality situated on the northern outskirts of Paris. The construction will extend for ?320? km and cover an area of 85,000 m^2 on a site easily accessible by the road and rail system. In fact the area of Tartres, chosen to house the centre, is located on the edge of the capital, between the RD28 and Avenue Emile Zola, in the vicinity of the university and well-connected with various national research institutes. The intervention was commissioned in 2005 by the French Ministry of Culture and Communication from the Fuksas Studio, winner of the international competition. The idea submitted stems from a careful interpretation of the urban and natural surroundings and sets out to give a recognizable identity back to a landscape forgotten by architecture, but inhabited ion a daily basis by the local community. Thus the project aims to create a piece of city, to transform a space without any particular qualities into an attractive place to visit and live in, able to act as a magnet and generator of new creative tensions.

The complex consists of two basic parts: a large translucent container that houses the administrative offices, reception and conference areas; and the lower volumes, housing the archives themselves and the large reading room, under which is set the car park for 161 vehicles. The first block is faced with an aluminium "skin" pierced by a pattern of holes through which light enters the rooms set aside for study, while the other spaces open onto the outside through large expanses of transparent glass. The static quality of the main structure contrasts with the rhythm of the sequence of suspended volumes projecting towards the water, which seem to be endlessly multiplied in a continuous series of reflections.

The light reflected from the water, the tints of the trees, the rays of the sun and the landscape outside enter the building through the openings and the unbroken glass walls. Thus the design expresses the poetics of lightness by playing with the light, water, transparencies and colours, exploiting the changes over the course of the seasons thanks in part to the attention paid to the choice of vegetation planted out.

1. *Study sketches*

2. *Area plan*

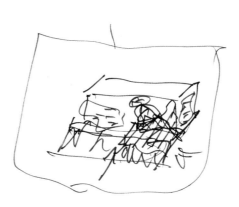

3. *View of the main front and the entrance
for the public*

4. *Models, view from above*

5. *Model, main view*

Masterplan Banci, Prato Area (Italy)

1. *Study model*

2. *General plan*

3-4. *Views of the conference-exhibition centre*

The study covers an area of 30 hectares that serves as a hinge between the consolidated aggregate of the historic city and the new residential and manufacturing extensions of the Badie and the Macrolotto.

The new urban layout, which has emerged over the course of meetings with the local government, develops the idea of Prato as a city undergoing transformation that has to find a prospect of its own for the future, with interventions that will unleash its economic and productive potentialities. Into this perspective fits the need to create a "Platform of Services" integrated with the realization of an important conference-exhibition centre and a hotel with a high standard of accommodation. This is combined with the reuse of a building of the Bigagli smelting works which will house the extension of the Museo di Arte Contemporanea Pecci.

Thus the intervention envisages a centre providing services on an interregional and national scale, inserted in a calibrated urban context and connected with the reality of the city. The urban project also sets out to knit together the break formed by the bypass known as the Declassata and the Banci industrial plant. Hence the following have been realized: a large public park of 8 hectares near the district of Le Badie; a central axis with themed gardens covering 6 hectares as well as an excellent set of parking facilities that will be located partly underground and partly above ground within interventions of landscaping to articulate the surface. The Exhibition-Conference Centre, together with the 60-m high hotel, constitutes the heart of the intervention. The project comprises an area of 13,000 m of exhibition space plus around 5000 m of services. The exhibition level is raised above the ground, freeing the area beneath to form a large covered plaza suited to public events and concerts.

Thus the platform of services is completed with a complex of buildings structured along a central pedestrian axis, which will house administrative functions (including new institutional offices) and ancillary commercial functions.

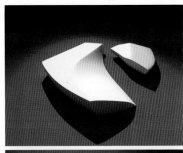

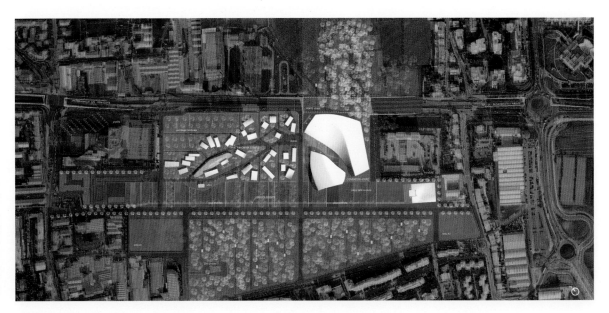

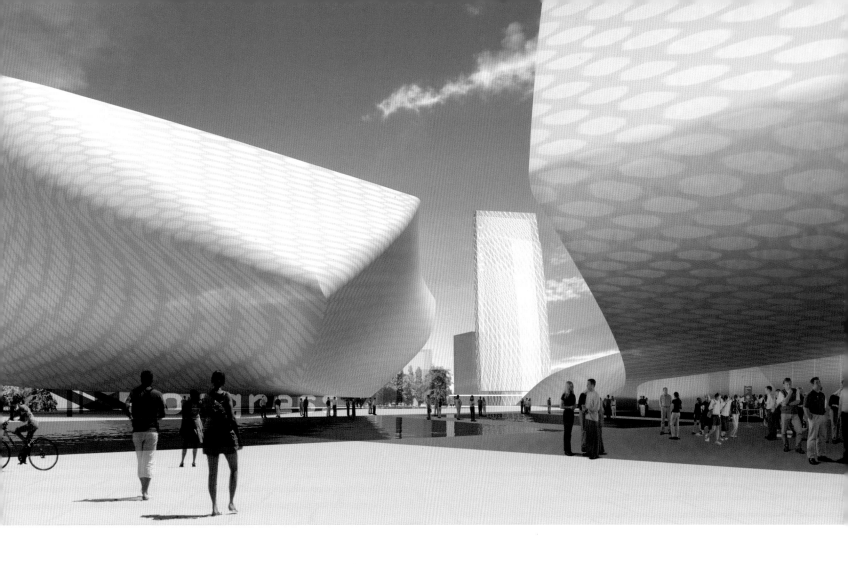

Vilnius Baltic Centre (Lithuania)

Vilnius Baltic Centre has a prime location by the river Neris between the old city and a busy street junction in Vilnius, Lithuania's capital city. The proposed integrated urban development includes three key elements: the Stadium, the Conference Centre and a central square which lays between them. The scheme links the Old Town Centre northbound to the river. At the Southern end of a pedestrian route linking the entire centre one encounters a 20,000 m² Conference and Congress Centre, a 400 bed five Star Hotel and a central semi-covered civic space, commercial and office space. Under the elegant shell-shaped roof of the Conference Centre lays a multipurpose entrance hall, conference rooms and a main auditorium creating the ideal space for international meetings.

The Stadium, designed as a "city arena" where different events can be hold, lays beyond the Central Piazza, with residential development to the East side of the sport centre. Sport related spaces are located around the stadium.

The concept idea originates from the central square, which is conceived as a meeting space both for the complex and the city. Retail spaces embrace the main buildings at ground floor level. The "shopping experience" flows reaching every corner of the site creating a dynamic atmosphere which the community will be part of.

In the same way that the "fluid of shops" fills the voids, the fragmentised roof links the main two poles of the project. The cover merges with the ground floor at the central point of the *piazza* incorporating to its structure the restaurant court over the public space.

The Congress Centre and the Hotel overlooking the river and opposite to the medieval castle represent a city landmark emphasizing the significance of the Vilnius Baltic Centre.

1. *General plan*

2-3. *Views of the Conference and Congress Centre and of the Stadium*

4. *Study sketch*

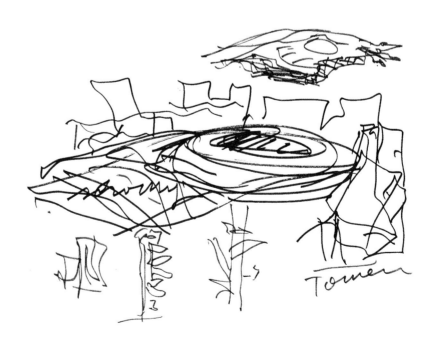

In just a few months Massimiliano Fuksas has inaugurated three works representing the conclusion of the Italian projects that mark the key second phase of his thirty years of experience as an architect.

The Ferrari Research Centre in Maranello, the Nardini "bubbles" in Bassano del Grappa and finally the new Fair in Milan compose an important and significant triad from various standpoints, effectively representing themes and problems of the contemporary Italian scene.

These are projects that fully express Fuksas' final phase of formal and spatial research and are apparently very distinct from the first, dense and very (geographically) localised Italian phase.

After the metaphors narrated in stone, steel and reinforced concrete of Paliano, Civita Castellana, Anagni and Orvieto, the recommencement came in 1995; the year of reopening of the Roman studio, to be precise, with a small work built in Frascati for the restoration of the Aldobrandini stables as an exhibition space. The context is very similar, but the design choices, materials and forms are very different, simpler yet more sophisticated, with all the arsenal of literature and ideology that accompanied the first works now absent, the relationship with the old construction more aware.

Yet this was just the beginning; this small, delicate intervention was followed by the unstoppable phase of national and local competitions that led to the victories for the Porta Palazzo building and the skyscraper of the Piedmont Regional Administration in Turin, to the EUR Auditorium and the ASI for Rome, the Ferrari Centre in Maranello, the church of S. Giacomo in Foligno, the new Fair in Milan, restoring the figure of a different, international architect, established and aware of his role, with a new language apparently light years away from his early works, an uninhibited communicator whose social role was reinforced by his appointment as director of the 2000 Biennial of Architecture; thanks to the themes and new authors involved, that particular Biennial did not leave its visitors indifferent, as has unfortunately happened with the following two editions.

A diverse author, because in the middle we have the decisive phase of French design and production, which showed us a personality particularly in his relations with production processes, in his mental attitude towards the project and in his relationships with the client, the general contractor and the enterprise. In my view it is no coincidence that at this moment, in Italy, three architects who have met with professional success and who have above all managed to win important competitions against tough competition from colleagues abroad and against the provincialism that often dominates our juries, all spent a long period working in France in the eighties and nineties. The presence today, in Italy, of Massimiliano Fuksas, Renzo Piano and Italo Rota is extremely healthy; they are like antibodies in relation to a resistant system that struggles to change pace and mentality in its now necessary relationship with Europe and a production and market system that have completely changed.

The small Nardini complex, for example, was created following a project with high technological and production quality expectations, but with the continued objective of relying entirely on the businesses and craftsmen present within a radius of thirty kilometres from the construction site. The work, of excellent quality, is there for all to see.

The Ferrari Research Centre came about following the desire of president Luca Cordero di Montezemolo to endow Ferrari, with its uncontested image of good design and great technology, with an industrial campus that was up to their standard, demonstrating that now, also in terms of marketing and not only of elementary quality of the space, good architecture is a necessary element of communication for the client and their production philosophy. The Fuksas project is the result of an international competition won in 1999 and completed in less than four years, together with three other new buildings by other authors.

The new Fair in Milan, on the other hand, is the most striking result in terms of its relationship between production and design quality, the winning project in a competition linking General Contractor and designer (in this particular case, the Astaldi group and Fuksas) with the obligation of delivering the work in thirty months. For these two years the work (total area 1.000.000 m²) has been the largest private worksite in Europe, filled with a multiethnic population of more than three thousand staff, including blue-collar workers, technicians and office staff, supported by a production network of European businesses and suppliers for a work of undisputed excellence.

The work has had an extraordinary echo worldwide, relaunching the image of the country, and Milan in particular, demonstrating two fundamental things: that things can be done in Italy too, done well and on schedule. Furthermore, that the substantial difference between the graceless and pathetic forms of Malpensa Airport, the true gate of entry to the city from the rest of the world, and the Milan Fair, lies in the capacity of the client in the latter case to focus on the work of a fine architect and on the formal quality of the spaces. Quality pays in terms of environmental comfort for the user, communication and medium-long term investment.

The three works by Fuksas are therefore significant, not only in terms of the designer's personal biography but also because they clearly show some of the confines within which we must move over the coming years if we want Italian architecture to have a new – and necessary – future. Italian architecture must return to being the bearer of new proposals that are visionary in cultural and project terms, combined with an unprecedented capacity to listen to the new demands that society is expressing; the designer must acquire awareness of his own social role and also become the bearer of demands for quality and excellence in relation to the client and above all in relation to the production system; paradoxically, Italian architecture must return to reflecting culturally on the concepts – not separate – of landscape and of heritage understood as complex unities, in which the place of tradition and the results of the post-war decades are finally reconciled.

Good Italian architecture, with its works, must help society become reconciled with the sophisticated concept of modernity, understood no longer as a rigid and superficial opposition between old and new, but now as a heterogeneous and complex system of spaces, values, images that today compose the national physical and social reality, undergoing a significant but unstoppable metamorphosis.

And for this country the works completed or under construction in recent years represent a fundamental test bench and at the same time a key opportunity. The long and laborious construction of the Auditorium in Rome by Renzo Piano finally showed that in Italy too it is possible to build a large new public work in a city that is difficult from the environmental standpoint, as is Rome, and the success of the building in public and image terms clearly demonstrates the sense and weight of a social demand, even before the existing one of politics and image. Together Piano's Auditorium and then Fuksas' Fair are showing on one hand the need for well informed, aware clients, well equipped to meet diverse challenges, considering the drowsy administrative and managerial system of our public authorities, and on the other the capacity of the system to equip itself quickly to meet new challenges (the thirty months of the Fair seem a mirage compared to the almost ten years for the management and realisation of the Auditorium).

Now a third large work, this too the result of a large international competition won by Fuksas, follows ideally the destiny of the earlier two: the new auditorium in Rome at the EUR, which should commence in the next few months, takes up the challenge in terms of construction quality, administrative efficiency and Fuksas' personal career path. Probably the most ambitious and difficult work so far conceived by the Roman architect, who faced the arduous task of giving finished, calibrated and controlled form to a dream, that cloud encapsulated in the large rational enclosure of steel and glass, the image of which first made the jury dream and now gives hope to the administration that has desired it so strongly and to a whole city, who see the materialisation of an impossible dream.

Yet this image also expresses the sense of what it means to build a new monument for a great metropolis. The size, the visionary aspect, the dream, the technological mystery, the emotions, the construction technique, the materials, the excellence of the spaces, the changing relationship with nature and the seasons, all these elements interact to transform a large building into a collective work, shared, reported and transmitted without the need for useless explanations.

A large worksite can become a gymnasium, and also a place of reflection for a whole generation of designers, not to transform the language into that of the academe (there is no cloud equal to the other...) but to reflect on the processes under way, on the relationship between modernity and context, on the need for and the civil value of good contemporary architecture. It is no coincidence that many of the new players on the Italian scene have passed through Fuksas' large Roman studio (from the Metrogramma, to Ian+, N! and Nemesi) to strengthen the new, necessary cultural and social role that he has acquired within Italian contemporary architectural culture, to be one of the necessary bridges between a national context that is rich but still very unaware of its real potential and an international dimension that is still very curious about what happens and is produced in Italy.

All these reflections bring me in the end to a question that I often wonder about, when observing the recent works of Massimiliano Fuksas: can we define Fuksas as an Italian author or a designer in whom the international dimension has definitely gained the upper hand, delivering his language and his works to the rather sterile Olympus of the dominant Neo-International Style?

I believe his destiny, based on his own experience and with his choices, is precisely to undergo a necessary metamorphosis that will increasingly see the expression of a complex contemporary national identity be defined not from a style or from the obsessive use of a local material, but rather from a precise mental attitude, from the basic choices that shape the project, from the relationship with light, materials, land and landscape, from a vision of the urban space and its intrinsic wealth, from its capacity to be rooted to the ground, to express it and also offer new visions, from the experience that enables technology to strengthen the space without commanding it and from the awareness that only man, with his concrete and fragile scale, can measure with his gestures the space where he is to live.

Annotated bibliography

M. Fuksas, A.M. Sacconi and S. Matta, *La scuola materna di Tarquinia*, Carte Segrete, Rome 1983.
M. Fuksas and A.M. Sacconi, *Architetture 1971-1983*, Faculté d'Architecture de Lille, Lille 1983.
M. Fuksas and A.M. Sacconi, *Da una casa... a un'altra ed altre storie di architettura dal 1983 al 1986*, Carte Segrete, Rome 1986.
Fuksas, catalogue of the exhibition *Dessins di Massimiliano Fuksas*, Architecture Art Galerie, Geneva, April-May 1988.
M. Pisani, *Fuksas, architetto*, Gangemi Editore, Rome 1988.
P. Goulet, *Herouville-Saint-Clair, Une Tour Européenne*, Carte Segrete, Rome 1988.
A. Bonito Oliva, 'Massimiliano Fuksas,' in *Blue Lagoon*, no. 6, Carte Segrete, Rome 1990.
P. Goulet, *Massimiliano Fuksas, Hambourg*, Carte Segrete, Paris 1990.
A. Greco, *Fuksas, Blue Town*, Carte Segrete, Rome 1990.
M. Fuksas, J.M. Sens and H. Tonka, *La & ailleurs, vingt-cinq années d'architecture. Massimiliano Fuksas*, Pandora Editions, Paris 1991.
J.M. Sens, H. Tonka, *La Maison de la Communication. De Massimiliano Fuksas à Saint-Quentin-en-Yvelines*, Pandora, Paris 1991.
P. Goulet, *Massimiliano Fuksas 60 Projets*, Institut Français d'Architecture, Carte Segrete, Rome 1992.

M. Fuksas, *Downtown. 1992-94*, Carte Segrete, Rome 1994.
M. Fuksas, *Neue Bauten und Projekte/Recent Buildings and Projects*, Artemis, Zurich 1994.
M. Fuksas, *Un jour... une ville!*, Conférences d'Architectes, Pavillon de l'Arsenal, Editions Pavillon de l'Arsenal, Paris 1994-1995.
R. Lenci and Massimiliano Fuksas. *Oscillazioni e Sconfinamenti*, Testo & Immagine, Turin 1996.
Massimiliano Fuksas, *One. Zero Architectures*, Giorgio Mondadori, Rome 1997.
Massimiliano Fuksas, Editions du Regards, Paris 1997.
Massimiliano Fuksas, CAW Contemporary World Architects, Rockport Publishers, Gloucester 1998.
Massimiliano Fuksas, in *L'Arca Plus*, no. 21, April 1999, L'Arca, Milan.
Less Aesthetics more Ethics, catalogue of the VII International Exhibition of Architecture, Venice Biennale, Marsilio, Venice 2000.
City: Third Millennium, International Competition of Ideas, Marsilio, Venice 2000.
Massimiliano Fuksas, Occhi chiusi aperti, Alinea, Florence 2001.
M. Fuksas and P. Conti, *Caos Sublime*, Rizzoli, Milan 2001.
M. Fuksas, *Frames*, Actar, Barcelona 2001.
M. Fuksas and Doriana Mandrelli, *Emporio Armani – Chater House, Hong Kong*, Actar, Barcelona 2004.

List of works represented

Sport Palace
concept
1970
realization
1973
location
Sassocorvaro (Pesaro Urbino, Italy)
customer
Sassocorvaro Municipality
designer
Massimiliano Fuksas
design team
A.M. Sacconi

San Giorgetto School
concept
1975
realization
1975-1986
location
Anagni (Frosinone, Italy)
customer
Anagni Municipality
designer
Massimiliano Fuksas con Anna Maria Sacconi
design team
G. Micheli, S. Crisanti

"Fontana del Diavolo" Park
concept
1977
realization
1978
location
Paliano (Frosinone, Italy)
customer
Paliano Municipality
designer
Massimiliano Fuksas with Anna Maria Sacconi
design team
G. Micheli, S. Crisanti

Nursery-school
concept
1977
realization
1978-1982
location
Tarquinia (Viterbo, Italy)
customer
Tarquinia Municipality
designer
Massimiliano Fuksas with Anna Maria Sacconi
design team
G. Micheli, S. Crisanti

New Cemetery
concept
1977
realization
1980-1990
location
Paliano (Frosinone, Italy)
customer
Paliano Municipality
designer
Massimiliano Fuksas with Anna Maria Sacconi
design team
G. Micheli, S. Crisanti

Nursery-school
concept
1979
realization
1979-1982
location
Paliano (Frosinone, Italy)
customer
Paliano Municipality
designer
Massimiliano Fuksas with Anna Maria Sacconi
design team
G. Micheli, S. Crisanti

Gymnasium
concept
1979
realization
1979-1985
location
Paliano (Frosinone, Italy)
customer
Paliano Municipality
designer
Massimiliano Fuksas with Anna Maria Sacconi
design team
G. Micheli, S. Crisanti

Sport Center
concept
1979
realization
1980-1986
location
Anagni (Frosinone, Italy)
customer
Anagni Municipality
designer
Massimiliano Fuksas
design team
S. Crisanti, G. Micheli

New Municipality seat
concept
1980
realization
1980-1990
location
Cassino (Italy)
customer
Comune di Cassino
designer
Massimiliano Fuksas with Anna Maria Sacconi
design team
G. Micheli, G. Desmet, L. Reyn

Cemetery extension
concept
1984
realization
1984-1991
location
Orvieto (Italy)
customer
Comune di Orvieto (Terni)
designer
Massimiliano Fuksas with Anna Maria Sacconi
design team
G. Micheli, S. Crisanti, A. Pace

Cemetery
concept
1985
realization
1985-1992
location
Civita Castellana (Viterbo, Italy)
customer
Civita Castellana Municipality
designer
Massimiliano Fuksas with Anna Maria Sacconi
design team
G. Micheli, M. Magee

Cultural center and library
concept
1986
realization
1987-1991
location
Rezé (France)
customer
Rezé Municipality
designer
Massimiliano Fuksas with Anna Maria Sacconi
design team
P. Basse, G. Micheli, S. Crisanti, P. Collier,
G. Desmet, M. Magee

Ilot Candie-Saint-Bernard
project competition winner
concept
1987
realization
1988-1996
location
Paris XI (France)
customer
RIVP (Régie immobilière del la Ville de Paris)
designer
Massimiliano Fuksas with Anna Maria Sacconi
design team
G. Desmet (head project), G. Micheli, S. Crisanti,
P. Collier, M. Magee, D. Gester, P. McDonough

Museum of Graffiti
project competition winner
concept
1988
realization
1989-1993
location
Niaux (France)
customer
Conseil Général de l'Ariège
designer
Massimiliano Fuksas
landscape designer
F. Zagari, A. Marguerit
design team
I. Capia, J.L. Fulerand, G. Zordan, F. Zagari

**Institut Européen d'Aménagement
et d'Architecture (INEAA)**
project competition winner
concept
1989
realization
1990-1993
location
Rouen (France)
customer
Ragion de Haute-Normandie
designer
Massimiliano Fuksas
design team
V. Morgan (head project), P. Caruso, D. Turci

Saint-Exupéry college

project competition winner

concept
1989
realization
1990-1993
location
Noisy-le-Grand (France)
customer
Conseil général de la Seine-Saint-Denis
et SODEDAT 93
designer
Massimiliano Fuksas
design team
P. Anania, G. Bellaviti, P. Caruso, M. Constantin,
P. Vitale

Law and Economic sciences Faculty

project competition winner

concept
1989
realization
1990-1996
location
Limoges (France)
customer
Ministero Nazionale dell'Educazione
designer
Massimiliano Fuksas
design team
P. Caruso, G. Desmet (head project), Mirala
Constantin, Aimé Djourno, F. Hansoul

**Former Aldobrandini Stables, now Museo
del Tuscolo**

concept
1989-1997
realization
1998-2000
location
Frascati (Rome, Italy)
customer
Frascati Municipality
designer
Massimiliano Fuksas with Doriana Mandrelli
design team
Lorenzo Accapezzato (head project)

University of the Centre Ville

international project competition winner

concept
1992
realization
1993-1994
location
Brest (France)
customer
Communauté Urbaine de Brest
designer
Massimiliano Fuksas
design team
R. Nishimori (head project)

Maison des Arts

project competition winner

concept
1992
realization
1993-1995
location
Bordeaux (France)
customer
Conseil Régional d'Aquitaine
designer
Massimiliano Fuksas
design team
P. Anania (head project)

Fuksas Studio

concept
1993
realization
1993
location
Rome (Italy)
customer
Massimiliano Fuksas with Doriana Mandrelli
designer
Massimiliano Fuksas with Doriana Mandrelli

Europark 1

international project competition winner

concept
1994
realization
1994-1997
location
Salzburg (Austria)
customer
Spar Warenhandela AG
designer
Massimiliano Fuksas
design team
C. Schepis, D. Haupt (head project), J. Machado,
R. Lanning, B. Kaijser, F. Tranfa, J. Woelk,
P. Anania, J. Kirimoto, J. Sato, G. Di Gregorio,
S. Delisi, A. Viola, E. Fuksas

Lycée Maximilien Perret De Vincennes

project competition winner

concept
1995
realization
1995-1998
location
Alfortville (France)
customer
Région de l'Île de France
designer
Massimiliano Fuksas
design team
P. Anania, A. Armagan (Capoprogetto)

**Urban reorganization of the Place
des Nations**

international project competition winner

concept
1995
realization
1995-1999
location
Geneva (Switzerland)
customer
Départ des Travaux publiques et de l'énergie,
République et Canton de Genève, ONU,
Gouvernement Fédéral, l'OMPI, l'UIT, l'Université
de Genève
designer
Massimiliano Fuksas
design team
1ª fase: C. Schepis (head project), C. Dattilo,
P. Anania, E. Fuksas, G.Micheli, A. Viola,
P. Matteuzzi, G. Di Gregorio, D. Vesper
2ª fase: N. Meystre, E. Greco (head project), F. De
Luca, F. Lonzano Lalinde, M. Mazzoli, F. Caccavale

Twin Towers / Masterplan Wienerberg city

international project competition winner

concept
1995
realization
1999-2001
location
Vienna (Austria)
customer
Wienerberger Baustoffindustrie AG;
Immofinanz Immobilien Anlagen AG
designer
Massimiliano Fuksas
design team
studio roma: A. Casadei, A. Hahne (head project)
C. Baglivo, F. Caccavale, R.Crespi, F. Lozano
Lalinde, T. Noske, K. Onori, C. Schenck,
M. Schmidt-Rabenau
studio roma: R. Bock (head project)
J. Behrens, S. Bruno, E.U. Faix, M. Kavalirek,
Z. Kiss, J. Mandl, B. Schwering

**Arbeiten am Alsterfleet; Wohnen Am
Alsterfleet**

project competition winner

concept
1997
realization
2001-2002
location
Hamburg (Germany)
customer
Quantum Immobilien AG, Hanseatische Projektier
Ungsgesellschaft mbH
designer
Massimiliano Fuksas
design team
T.P. Brendel (head project), J. Knaack, T. Stiller,
M. Witzmann, V. Schreieder, M. Abadir,
E. Brutzkus, C. Weinecke, A. Kudla

Peace Center

concept
1997
realization
2003-2006
location
Jaffa (Israel)
customer
Simon Peres
designer
Massimiliano Fuksas
design team
A. Casadei, F. Bastoni, K. Sullivan, T. Balbaa,
T. Mota Saraiva

Competition for a synagogue, cultural centre and offices
international competition
concept
1997
location
Dresden (Germany)
customer
Jüdiche Gemeinde zu Dresden
designer
Massimiliano Fuksas
design team
M. Jocham (head project), F. Lonzano, M. Mazzoli,
E. Greco, F. Caccavale, D. Effmert, M. Mesa, G. Poli

Hansforum and Alsterfleet
project competition winner
concept
1998
realization
2001-2002
location
Hamburg (Germany)
customer
Conferenza Episcopale Italiana - Diocesi di Foligno
designer
Massimiliano Fuksas
design team
T.P. Brendel (head project), J. Knaack, T. Stiller, M.
Witzmann, M. Abadir, E. Brutzkus,
C. Weinecke, A. Kudla, D. Goesmann

New Clothing Pavilion at Porta Palazzo
project competition winner
concept
1998
realization
2001-2006
location
Turin (Italy)
customer
Città di Torino
designer
Massimiliano Fuksas
design team
R. Gaggi (head project), F. Caccavale,
C. Gagliardi, L. La Torre, S. Martino, A. Savino

Palazzo Centro Congressi EUR
international project competition winner
concept
1998
realization
2001-2007
location
Rome-Eur (Italy)
customer
Rome Municipality with Eur CCI S.p.A.
(Centro Congressi Italia)
designer
Massimiliano Fuksas
design team
competition Ist stage: F. Cibinel, G. Lacognata,
A. Ricci (Capoprogetto)
competition IInd stage: A. Casadei, F. Cibinel
(Capoprogetto)
preliminary design stage:
L. Accapezzato; F. Cibinel (head project),
F. Caccavale, L. Peralta, T. Saikawa, C. Baccarini,
D. Binarelli, F. Boin, A. D'Amico, M. Teresa
Facchinetti, T. Hegemann, K. Nogami, A. Savino,
F. Semproni, M. Takada
final design stage:
L. Accapezzato, A. Ghirardelli (head project)
C. Floris, R. Laurenti, T. Yamaguchi, P. Barone,
D. Biondi, F. Giancola, E. Taranta, A. Pio Saracino

Competition for a stadium
international project competition winner
concept
1998
location
Salzburg (Austria)
customer
SWS Wals-Siezenheim
designer
Massimiliano Fuksas
design team
F. Cibinel, F. Bacillari, F. D'Agnano

Mall and casino extension
international project competition winner
concept
1998
realization
1999-2004
location
Eindhoven (Netherlands)
customer
William Properties
designer
Massimiliano Fuksas
design team
G. Pyckevet, T. Broekaert (head project),
K. Sullivan, M. Crò, F. Polacchi, T. Balbaa, C. Peña,
J. Lindenthal, M. Stahlmann, T. Mota Saraiva

Competition for Berna Hall
international project competition winner
concept
1999
location
Brünnen-Berna (Austria)
customer
Genossenshaft Migros Aare
designer
Massimiliano Fuksas
design team
F. Cibinel, C.Baccarini, H. Mendoza, F. Sacconi,
T. Balbaa

7th Venice Biennale
concept
2000
realization
2000
location
Venice (Italy)
director
Massimiliano Fuksas
video-installation
284m x 5m
adaptation and production
Massimiliano Fuksas, Doriana Mandrelli

Ferrari operational headquarters
concept
2000
realization
2001-2003
location
Maranello (Modena, Italy)
customer
Ferrari S.p.a.
designer
Massimiliano Fuksas
design team
G. Martocchia (head project), F. Cibinel, D. Dilber
Stolfi, A. Savino, D. Binarelli
interior design
Doriana Mandrelli

Competition for the headquarters of the Italian Space Agency
international project competition winner
concept
2000
location
Rome (Italy)
customer
Agenzia Spaziale Italiana
designer
Massimiliano Fuksas
design team
L. Accapezzato (head project), F. Cibinel,
S. Martino, R. Gaggi, C. Baccarini, D. Binarelli,
A. D'amico, M.T. Facchinetti, C. Gagliardi,
K. Nogami, M. Takada

San Giacomo parish complex
international project competition winner
concept
2000
realization
2001-2007
location
Foligno (Perugia, Italy)
customer
Conferenza Episcopale Italiana - Diocesi di Foligno
designer
Massimiliano Fuksas
design team
G. Martocchia, (head project), K. Kimizuka,
D. Biondi, F. Cibinel, S. Maio, P. Barone, T. Balbaa,
T. Mota Saraiva.

New concept per Armani
concept
2001
realization
2001-2002
location
Hong Kong (Cina)
customer
Giorgio Armani
designer
Massimiliano Fuksas with Doriana Mandrelli
design team
D. Stolfi (head project), I. Wadham , D. Dilber,
M. Takada, N. Cabiati

Europark 2-Inseln
concept
2001
realization
2005
location
Salzburg (Austria)
customer
Europark Errichtungsges.M.B.H.
designer
Massimiliano Fuksas
design team
T. Hegemann, A. Ghirardelli (head project),
A. Kreft, Gijs Pyckevet, F. Arrigon, L. Fornari,
D. Raptus, M. Stahlmann, F. Bucchieri, S. Pir,
N. Francula, D. Marchetti, M. Iovanel, F. Mosciatti,
S. Dotlic, C. Baccarini

De Cecco Management Centre
international competition
concept
2001
realization
2005-2007
location
Pescara (Italy)
customer
De Cecco S.p.a.
designer
Massimiliano Fuksas
design team
L. Accapezzato (head project), A. Ghirardelli,
S. Wood, G. Pyckevet, C. Floris, M. Motolese

Competition for the new seat of regional government in Piedmont, the Palazzo della Regione Piemonte
project competition winner
concept
2001
location
Turin (Italy)
customer
Regione Piemonte
designer
Massimiliano Fuksas
design team
F. Cibinel, F. Caccavale, G. Marmocchia,
D. Binarelli, L. Pistoia, S. Martino

Nardini Exhibition Centre and Auditorium
concept
2002
realization
2002-2004
location
Bassano del Grappa (Vicenza, Italy)
customer
Ditta Bortolo Nardini S.p.A.
designer
Massimiliano Fuksas
design team
C. Baccarini, D. Stolfi, D. Dilber, L. Maugeri,
I. Wadham
interior design
Doriana Mandrelli

New Trade Fair Rho-Pero
international project competition winner
concept
2002
realization
2002-2005
location
Rho-Pero (Milan, Italy)
customer
Fondazione Fiera Milano
General contractor
Astaldi Spa, Vianini Spa, Pizzarotti Spa
Central axis sail
Structural designer
Mero GmbH & Co.
Structural consultant
Schlaich Bergermann und Partner
Service centre logo
Structural designer
Schlaich Bergermann und Partner
Designer e art director
Doriana O. Mandrelli

Architectural project managers
Giorgio Martocchia, Ralf Bock
3D
Fabio Cibinel
design team
Angelo Agostani, Fabrizio Arrigoni, Chiara Baccarini,
giulio Baiocco, Daniele Biondi, Giuseppe Blengini,
Laura Buonfrate, Sofia Cattinari, Irene Ciampi, Chiara Costanzelli, Alberto Greti, Kentaro Kimizuca, Roberto Laurenti, Davide Marchetti, Luca Maugeri, Dominique Raptis, Cesare Rivera, Adele Savino, Tasja Tesche, Toyohiko Yamaguchi
Model
Gianluca Brancaleone (project leader), Nicola Cabiati, Andrea Fornello, Andrea Marazzi, Andy Dovizia.
Constructional engineers for central axis, service centre
Studio Marzullo

Conference centre
concept
2002
realization
2004-2007
location
Frankfurt am Main (Germany)
customer
MAB Zeil Forum GmbH & Co KG
designer
Massimiliano Fuksas
design team
G. Pyckevet, S. Dotlic (head project), F. Cibinel,
D. Marchetti, C. Baccarini

New concept for Armani
concept
2003
realization
2003-2004
location
Shanghai (China)
customer
Giorgio Armani
designer
Massimiliano Fuksas with Doriana Mandrelli
design team
D. Stolfi (head project), I. Wadham

Armani Jeans-Milan
concept
2003
realization
2003-2004
location
Milan (Italy)
customer
Giorgio Armani
designer
Massimiliano Fuksas with Doriana Mandrelli
design team
D. Stolfi (head project), I. Wadham, N. Cabiati

Zenith competition
project competition winner
concept
2003
realization
2005-2006
location
Strasbourg (France)
customer
Città di Strasburgo
designer
Massimiliano Fuksas
design team
E. Amantea (head project), F. Cibinel,
G. Martocchia, R. Laurenti, J. Gelez, F. Duchêne,
A. Kudla, L. Aquili, S. Wood, C. Baccarini

Exhibition centre
international project competition winner
concept
2003
location
Astana (Kazakhstan)
customer
City of Astana
designer
Massimiliano Fuksas
design team
L. Aquili, F. Cibinel, C. Knoll, M. Maurer,
R. Laurenti, M. Maurer, R. Laurenti

Competition, Salford
international project competition winner
concept
2004
realization
2008
location
Salford-Greater Manchester (Great Britain)
customer
Central Salford Urban Regeneration Company
designer
Massimiliano Fuksas
design team
C. Knoll (head project), F. Cibinel, R. Laurenti,
G. Wetzel

Stazione Duomo, Metropolitana
concept
2004
realization
2008
location
Naples (Italy)
customer
Metropolitana di Napoli S.p.a.
designer
Massimiliano Fuksas
design team
A. Savino, F. Arrigoni, G. Brancaleone,
G. Calcagno, S. Delle Piane

Olympic Aquatic Center
concorso internazionale
concept
2004
location
London (Great Britain)
customer
The London Development Agency
designer
Massimiliano Fuksas
design team
G. Martocchia, C. Knoll (head project), F. Cibinel,
R. Laurenti, A. Greti, D. Biondi, D. Raptus,
G. Wetzel, G. Cafaggini, N. Haim, F. Pitzalis

**Centre des Archives Nationales de
Pierrefitte-sur-Seine et Saint-Denis**
international project competition winner
concept
2005
realization
2006-
location
Pierrofitte-sur-Seine, Saint Denise (France)
customer
Ministro della Cultura e Comunicazione
designer
Massimiliano Fuksas with Doriana O. Mandrelli
landscape designer
F. Mercier
design team
G. Mastrocchia, V. Amantea (head project),
F. Cibinel. R. Laurenti, D. Biondi, D. Raptis.
G.Cafaggini, F. Portesine, T. Janka

Masterplan Area Banci
concept
2005
realization
2005/2010
location
Prato
designer
Massimiliano Fuksas with Doriana O. Mandrelli
design team
Gianluca Brancaleone, Lucio Campanelli, Andrea
Fornello, Frauke Stenz, Susanna Tundo, Fulvia
Tallini

Vilnius Baltic Center
concept
2005
realization
2005/2010
location
Vilnius (Lithuania)
customer
Ubig Bank
designer
Massimiliano Fuksas
design team
G. Martocchia, M. Suarez, F. Cibinel, A. Griggio,
R. Laurenti, D. Raptis, E. Theocharopoulon,
N. Cabiati

Main projects and realisations

2005-
Vilnius Baltic Center (Lituania)
2005-
Masterplan Area Banci (Prato)
2005-
Central State Archive in Paris, international competition, winning project
2005-2012
Olympic Aquatic Centre, London, international competition
2004-
Naples underground railway, Duomo station, Piazza Nicola Amore, Naples, Italy
2004-
Central Salford Vision and Regeneration Framework, Salford (Manchester), UK, international competition, winning project
2004
High-rise building with retail, office, hotel - Sankei building, Osaka, Japan, competition
2003-2004
New concepts for Emporium Armani, Showroom, Cafeteria, Restaurant, Shanghai, China
2003-2004
Armani Jeans, Porta Ticinese, Milan, Italy
2003-2006
Zenith concert hall, Strasbourg, France, winning project in competition
2003-
Exhibition centre, offices, restaurant, café, Astana, Kazakhstan, international competition, winning project
2003
Urban block with spaces for commerce, residences, offices, Mainz, Germany, competition, winning project
2003
Concept for shops, Palmers AG, Austria, competition
2003
Zenith concert hall, Amiens, France, competition, winning project
2003
Feasibility study, master plan and offices for the new Miroglio-Vestebene centre, Alba (Cuneo), Italy
2003
José Vasconcelos Central Library, Mexico City, Mexico, competition
2003
New National Archives, Luxembourg, competition by invitation
2003
100 homes, Paris, France, competition by invitation

2003
Urbanistic project, Hamburg, Germany, competition by invitation
2003
High school, Orestad Copenhagen, Denmark, competition by invitation
2003
Business centre and urbanistic project, Levji Grad, Slovenia, competition by invitation
2003
New centre for the Puglia Regional Council, Bari, Italy, competition
2003
Offices and exhibition area for Mobile Solution Centre, Bremen, Germany, competition by invitation
2003
Town hall in Montpellier, France, competition by invitation
2002-2008
MAB Zeil, shopping centre, offices, hotel, restaurants, fitness centre, Frankfurt, Germany
2002-2005
New Fair Pole, Rho-Pero, offices, pavilions, restaurants, facilities, Milan, Italy, competition, winning project
2002-2004
Restructuring and enlargement of the Bortolo Nardini company, Bassano del Grappa (Vicenza), Italy
2002
Tea & Coffee Tower, set for Alessi in collaboration with Doriana O. Mandrelli
2002
"Interni in Piazza" New space capsule, Milan Triennial, Italy
2002
Erlangen Arcaden, shopping centre, Erlangen, Germany
2002
Aquadeus, aquatic park, Salzburg, Austria
2002
Juventus Viaggi, travel agency, Rome, Italy
2002
Canal + Louveciennes, offices, campus, restaurants, hotel, meeting points, commerce, Louveciennes, Paris, France
2001-2007
De Cecco Business District, New offices, "FATER" S.p.A., Pescara, Italy
2001-2006
Enlargement of the Mall and Entertainment Centre, Europark "Inseln", Salzburg, Austria

2001-2003
Centre des Exposition et des Congrès, Angoulème, France, international competition, winning project
2001-2002
New concept for Emporium Armani, Hong Kong, China
2001-2003
New headquarters of the Süddeutschen Verlages publishing group, Versand Auslobungstext, Munich, Germany, international competition
2001-
Lyon confluence. Bassine Portuarie et centre de Loisirs, Lyon, France
2001-
San Giacomo parish complex, Foligno, Italy, international competition, winning project
2001-
New building for the Piedmont Regional Authority, Turin, Italy, winning project in international competition
2001-
Inner City Development in Prague 2001 (Docks Prague 8), offices and mall
2001
Handles for Valli e Valli with Doriana O. Mandrelli, Milan, Italy
2001
Queensland Gallery of Modern Art, Brisbane, Australia, international competition
2001
Justizzentrum, Aachen, Germany, international competition
2001
Study for a new concept of modern art gallery. Rome fashion week, Congress Building, Rome, Italy
2001
Studienauftrag Theilerplat Landis and Gyr Areal und Sbb West, Zug, Switzerland, international competition
2001
Office building. Am Sandtorkai, Hamburg, Germany, international competition
2001
Concept Plan competition for the development of an integrated arts, cultural and entertainment district at the West Kowloon Reclamation, Hong Kong, China, international competition
2000-2003
Multi-purpose Complex and Entertainment Centre, Belpasso, Catania, Italy
2000-2003
New business centre and Research centre for Ferrari S.p.A, Maranello (Modena), Italy

2000-2002
Residential centre, commerce, Rimini, Italy
2000-
New headquarters of the Italian Space Agency, Rome, Italy, international competition, winning project
2000
Residential complex, offices, cinema, service sector, Brachmüle, Vienna, Austria, international competition, winning project
2000
Urbanistic restructuring of the De la Source district, Orléans, France, competition
2000
Workshop Gießereigelände, shopping centre, congress centre, hotel, Ingolstadt, Germany, international competition
2000
New headquarters for Consiag, Prato, Italy, international competition, winning project
2000
Urban plan, Rogoredo (Milan), Italy
2000
Enlargement of the headquarters of the WIPO (World Intellectual Property Organisation), Geneva, Switzerland, international competition, 2nd prize
2000
Showroom degli Effetti, Rome, Italy
2000
VII Biennial of Architecture in Venice, "Less Aesthetics More Ethics", Italy
1999-2003
Residential and hotel centre, commerce, Valenza Po (Alessandria), Italy
1999-2002
Residential complex, Brescia, Italy
1999-2001
Equestrian Centre, Parc du Château Bleu Tremblay-en-France, France
1999
Freizeit-und-Einkaufszentrum, Bern, Switzerland, international competition, winning project
1999
TV-world, Hamburg, Germany, international competition, 3rd prize
1999
"World of Sport", Adidas, Hezogenaurach, Germany, international competition, project receiving mention
1999
Residential complex, offices, commerce, Pescara, Italy, international competition
1999
New railway station, Imperia, Italy, competition by invitation

1999
Sports complex, Chalon sur Saone, France
1999
Realization of a new district with public structures and green areas, Amiens, France, competition, winning project
1999
Residential complex, offices, hotel, Schönbrunn, Vienna, Austria, international competition
1999
Enlargement of the "Messe Zentrum", Salzburg, Austria, international competition
1998-2007
Congress Centre, Rome-Eur, Italy, international competition, winning project
1998-2006
New Clothing pavilion at Porta Palazzo, for the Municipality of Turin, Italy, competition by invitation winning project
1998-2004
Admirant, enlargement of the "Piazza" shopping centre and Mall, Eindhoven, Holland, international competition, winning project
1998-2004
Tourist port of Marina di Stabia, Naples, Italy
1998-2003
"Staircase to the stars", Bethlehem, Palestine, for Yasser Arafat
1998-2002
Building for offices, Hanse-Forum, Hamburg, Germany
1998-2002
Fue towers for residences, Milan, Italy, for Gruppo Finanziario Lombardo S.p.A.
1998
SWS Stadion, Salzburg Wals - Siezenheim, Salzburg, Austria, international competition, winning project
1998
"Usine pour le traitements des eaux", Caen, France, competition, winning project
1998
Plan for the urbanistic restructuring of Castellammare di Stabia (Naples), Italy
1998
Wohnungsbau Ost, Alte Messe, urbanistic layout designing for housing use of a part of the old Fair in Leipzig, Germany, international competition by invitation, winning project
1998
Brückenschlag und Reisegarten, Vlotho–Exter, Germany, international competition, winning project
1997-2006
Peres Center for Peace, Jaffa, Israel

1997-2002
Residences and offices on the Alsterfleet, Hamburg, Germany, international competition, winning project
1997-2002
Residential complex and offices for the Hanseatica DWI, Hamburg, Germany, competition, winning project
1997-2000
Project for the restoration and functional redevelopment of the Stazione Termini, Rome, Italy
1997
Lycée a Haute Qualité Environnementale, Caudry, France, competition
1997
New headquarters of the General Administration of Deutche Post Ag, Bonn, Germany, international competition by invitation
1997
Synagogue, cultural centre, offices, Dresden, Germany, competition
1997
Functional restructuring of the former Aquarium and Theatre for Vittorio Gassman, Rome, Italy
1997
New headquarters of the Caisse des Dépôts et Consignations, Paris, France, international competition by invitation
1997
"Via Triumphalis" 2022, urbanistic layout designing from the Schloßplatz to the Kongreszentrum in Karlsruhe, Germany, competition
1997
Realisation of a carless residential district in the area of the old " Hindenburg-Kaserne " in Münster, Germany, competition
1997
Furniture for Saporiti Italia, Milan, Italy, with Doriana O. Mandrelli
1997
Multimedia centre, Rotherbaum, Hamburg, Germany, international competition by invitation
1997
Preparation of displays for the XII National Quadriennial of Art, Rome, Italy
1997
Central Library, Promenade des Arts, Nice, France, international competition by invitation
1997
Architectural redevelopment of the "Rathauspassage Innsbruck", Innsbruck, Austria, international competition by invitation

1997
"Hotel du Département" of the Charente Maritime, La Rochelle, France, international competition by invitation
1996-2001
Restructuring and enlargement of the Ilot Cantagrel (residences, studios for artists and car parks), Paris XIII, France, winning project in competition
1996-1999
Residential complex, Clichy, France
1996
Theme park devoted to football, Torvaianica, Italy
1995-1998
Maximilien Perret de Vincennes Centre for Training and Research on Construction, Library, documentation centre, Auditorium, residences for teachers and students, Alfortville, Paris, France, international competition, winning project
1995-1999
Urbanistic layout designing of the Place des Nations, project for the Maison Universelle, new venue for GATT, the central library, two university and research institutes, for the "Maison des droits de l'homme et des droits humanitaires", for a centre of worship for the various religious faiths, Geneva, Switzerland, UN, international competition, winning project
1995-2001
Twin Towers, new headquarters for Wienerberger, two towers for offices, multiplex, restaurants, underground car parka, Vienna, Austria, international competition, winning project
1995
Offices, residences and factory for the production and distribution of computers and software, Hamburg, Germany, competition
1995
Urbanistic-architectural layout of the Tiburtina and Tuscolana railway areas and of the Tiburtina-Colombo rail and road connection axis, Rome, Italy, international consultation by invitation
1995
Feasibility study for the designing of an administrative-residential district (homes, offices, school, childcare facility), Wienerbergstrasse/Triesterstrasse, Vienna, Austria, competition in two phases, winning project
1995
Feasibility study (offices) for Wendenstrasse City-Sud, Hamburg, Germany, competition, winning project

1995
Urbanistic-landscaping study of the area surrounding the " Nordbahnhof ", Berlin, Germany, international competition by invitation
1995
Feasibility study for designing the layout of the railway station district, Padua, Italy
1995
Urbanistic restructuring of the district of the Neusser Strasse, Munich, Germany, international competition
1995
Proposals for the re-use of the former "Sudrum Leipzig" coalmines, Germany, international competition of ideas
1995
New headquarters for the Caisse Française de Développement, Paris, competition by invitation, project receiving mention
1995
Residential complex, Paris, France
1995
Construction of a hotel and casino in Ljubljana, Slovenia
1995
Master plan for the Wienerberger district, Vienna, Austria
1994-1998
Residences for students and car parks, Alfortville, France, with Doriana O. Mandrelli
1994-1997
Mall and Entertainment Centre, Eurospar car parks, Europark, Salzburg, Austria, international competition, winning project
1994-
Layout designing of Place Alphonse Fiquet, restructuring of the architectural complex built by Auguste Perrets, Amiens, France, international competition, winning project
1994
Covered Omnisports Complex, open air sports facilities, underground public car parks, Rueil-Malmaison, France, competition
1994
Master Plan of the areas situated to the South of the Centro Agro Alimentare, Bologna, Italy, international competition
1994
Construction of the Gutenberg High School, ZAC des Sarrazins-ZAC Créteil Parc, Crèteil (val de Marne) France. Competition

1993-2002
Urban plan for Tremblay en France (for an area of 1000 ha.) for an international district at the airport of Roissy-Charles de Gaulle, Paris, France, competition, winning project

1993-1995
Study to define the layout of the centre of the "vieux pays", Temblay-en-France, France, competition

1993
Studio Fuksas Associati, Piazza del Monte di Pietà, Rome, Italy

1993
Studies for the redevelopment of "Piazza dei Miracoli", Pisa, Italy, national competition

1993
Construction of a central barracks for the Fire Service, Montebelard (Doubs), France

1993
Project to design the layout of the Port of Clichy-la Garenne, Paris, France

1993
Construction of a dental care and treatment centre - La Paillade, for the Centre Hospitalier Universitarie (CHU), Montpellier (Hérault), France

1992-1994
University of the Centre Ville, library, university restaurant, Brest, France, international competition, winning project

1992-1997
Reconstruction and restoration of 4 towers from the '60s, Montreuil, France

1992-1997
Residential complex, Clichy-la Garenne, France

1992-1995
Maison des Arts, University of Bordeaux III, France-Université Michel de Montaigne, winning project in competition

1992-1995
Regeneration of the "Cité des Aigues Douces", Marseilles, France

1992
Construction of a property for use by the police and parking wardens, Orly (Val de-Marne), France, competition

1992
Urbanistic and architectural restructuring of the district of the Town Hall (library and students district), Limoges, France, competition, winning project

1992
Regional Centre for Music and Voice, Argenteuil, France, competition

1992
ZAC Berges-de-Seine, project for the new Cables de Lyon district, Clichy, France

1992
Urbanistic restructuring of the Grand Ensemble de Clichy-sous-Bois, Montfermeil, France

1992
Residential complex, Milan, Italy

1992
"Intelligent offices", Rennes (Ille-et-Vilaine), France

1992
"Passerelle Solferino", a pedestrian bridge on the Seine, Paris, France, competition

1992
Construction of the U.F.R., University of Nice, France, with Jean Louis Fulcrand, Jean Capia and Gui Jourdan, competition

1992
Congress centre and enlargement of the Sheraton Hotel, Salzburg, Austria, competition

1992
Project for the redevelopment of the Borgo di Castellazzo, restoration of Villa Arconati Crivelli and the surrounding areas, protection of the wooded and agricultural areas, car parks to support the new road system, Bollate, Italy

1992
"Buero und Gescaeftshaus Willhelmgalerie", Potsdam, Germany, international competition

1992
Residential centre, offices, sports centre, Tremblay-en-France, Paris

1992
"Parc des sport et Cité de l'Eau", Publier (Haute-Savoie), France, competition

1992
Auditorium for opera, Amneville, France, international competition

1992
Reconstruction and transformation of the old Villa Zottmann into a museum for the collections of the Carnuntinum Archaeological Museum, Bad Deutsch-Altenburg, Austria, competition

1992
Urbanistic restructuring of the Friedrichstrasse district and railway station (residences, offices, services), Berlin, Germany, competition

1992
Reconstruction of the "Domaine Bâti du Petit Arbois", in the programme of the Europole Méditerranéenne, Aix-Les-Milles, France, competition, winning project

1992
Restoration and transformation of the "Gare du Prado" into a district for offices, homes and shopping centre, Marseilles, France, competition

1991-1993
Private residence, Paris, France

1991-1996
Restoration and enlargement of the Hotel-Dieu, Tableres, France, competition

1991-1996
Project for a district of homes, offices and services along the Sprea, Berlin, Germany, competition

1991-1996
Sports complex, car park, homes, shopping centre, offices, for the R.I.V.P, Paris, France

1991-1996
Urbanistic layout designing of the Lu Jiazui International Trade Centre, Pudong, Shanghai, China, over an area of 4,000,000 m2, international consultation

1991-1993
Layout designing of the area of the old port of Nagasaki, Japan, international consultation

1991-
Restructuring of a theatre and a cinema, Catanzaro, Italy

1991
One of 11 towers, "a collection along the river", Frankfurt, Germany, competition, winning project

1991
Residential Complex, Argenteuil, France, competition

1991
Reconstruction and enlargement of the cultural centre, Chevilly-Larue (Val-de-Marne), France, competition

1991
Enlargement of the university, Saint-Etienne, France, competition

1991
Offices, residences, shops in the area of the old airport, Munich, Germany, competition

1991
Urbanistic restructuring of the district of the old station, offices, residences, services, Frankfurt, Germany, competition

1991
Motorway tollgate at the barrier of Eprunes (Seine-et-Marne), France, competition

1991
Offices and Car parks, Gabriel Péri operation, Clichy-la-Garenne (Hauts-de-Seine), France

1991
200 homes, Guyancourt, Saint-Quentin-en-Yvelines (Yvelines), France, competition

1991
260 homes, Argenteuil (Val-d'Oise), France, competition

1991
Landscaping of an area of 90 hectares,Brétigny-sur-Orge, France, competition

1991
Urbanistic restructuring, Port-de-Bouc, Marseilles, France

1991
Tourist centre, Mandatoriccio (Catanzaro), Italy

1991
Cultural centre and urbanistic layout designing, Quimper (Finistère), France, competition

1991
Health centre, Pizzeria-Lido (Catanzaro), Italy

1991
Training and Research Unit in Law, Economics and Sciences, University of Tours, France, competition

1991
Studio Fuksas Associati, Vicolo della Frusta, Rome, Italy

1991
Extension of the Training and Research Unit in Law and Letters, Dijon, France, competition

1991
Restructuring of the West entrance of the RN14, Franconville, France, consultation, winning project

1991
Offices and laboratories for the departmental technical services Valenton-Creteils, France, competition

1991
Residences, offices and shops in the district of the Old Port of Hamburg, Germany, competition, winning project

1990-1995
University residences, Hérouville Saint-Clair, France

1989-2000
Regeneration and transformation of the former Aldobrandini Stables into the Museo del Tuscolo and mediatheque, Frascati (Rome), Italy

1989-1996
Restoration, enlargement and transformation of the "Immeuble Turgot" into the Faculty of Law and Economic Sciences, Limoges, France, winning project in competition

1989-1993
College Saint-Exupéry, CES 600, Noisy-le-Grand (Sein-Saint-Denis), France, winning project in competition

1989-1993
Restoration, enlargement and transformation of the Couvent des Pénitents into the Institut Européen d'Aménagement et d'Architecture (INEAA), Rouen, France, competition, winning project

1989-1993
Apartment, Yvan & Marzia rue du Jour, 75002 Paris, France

1989-1992
Ecole Nationale d'Ingénieurs et Institut Scientifique, Enib-Isamor, Brest, France, competition, winning project

1989-1992
House and private studio of the architect Adriano Pace, Cotronei (Catanzaro), Italy with Adriano Pace

1989-1992
Layout designing of the district of the Old Port, Hamburg, Germany

1989-1992
Restructuring of the Luth district, Gennevilliers, France, competition, winning project

1989-1991
Maison du Cablage et de la Communication, the EDISON district of the station, at Saint-Quentin-en-Yvelines, France

1989-1991
Residences and offices, Argenteuil, France

1989-1991
Restructuring of the town centre, Allonnes, France, competition, winning project

1989-1991
Castorama Supermarket, Herouville-Saint-Clair, France

1989-1990
Sandtohoft-Kehrwieder, restructuring of the district of the old port, business centre, residences, offices, Hamburg, Germany, competition

1989
"Quai Branly" international conference and hotel centre, Paris, France, international competition

1989
Viaduct, urban project, Valmontone, Rome, Italy, competition, winning project

1989
Restructuring of the Bouilly-Pasteur sector of the Cochin hospital, Paris, France, competition

1989
New cemetery, Acquappesa, Catanzaro

1989
"Forum et Foyer" Centres for the National institute of Telecommunications, Evry (Esonne), France, competition

1989
Restructuring of the town centre, Montmorency (Val-d'Oise), France, competition

1989
Cultural centre, Saint Loubes (Gironde), France, competition

1989
Restructuring of a shopping centre, Limonest-Dardilliy (Rhône), France

1989
School complex, Platani district, Perpignan (Pyrénées-Orientale), France, competition

1989
Centre for arts, technologies and the media, Karlsruhe, Germany, competition with William Alsop

1989
Congress centre, Belfort, France

1989
Business and exhibition centre, Nalco district, Cisterna (Latina), Italy

1989
Intermunicipal funeral complex, Dijon, France, competition

1989
ENSMA (Ecole Nationale Supérieure de Mécanique et Aéronautique) Futuroscope, Poitiers, France, competition

1989
Restructuring of the banks of the Seine, Clichy-la-Garenne, France, competition, winning project

1989
Chamber of Commerce and Industry of Nîmes-Uzès-Le Vigan, Nîmes, France, competition, winning project with Jean Louis Fulcrand, Guy Giordan, Jean Capia

1989
Restructuring of two sectors, 3/11 West India Dock Road and 4-10 East Dock Road, Docklands, London, UK, international competition, winning project

1989
Urban restructuring of the town centre, Amiens, France, first, second and third phase

1989
Restructuring of the "Folies" district, Saint-Germain-les-Arpajon, France, competition

1989
Roof restaurant on the "Liberté" building, Argenteuil (Val-d'Oise), France

1989
Offices and Shops, Porte de Bezons, Bezons (val d'Oise), France

1989
Urbanistic regeneration of the former Nalco site, Cisterna (Latina), Italy

1989
National Conservatory of Music and Dance, Reims, France, competition

1989
Restructuring of the banks of the Rhone, Valence, France, international consultation

1989
International centre for fashion, Tremblay-en-France, France

1989
Enlargement of the ENITIAA, Nantes, France, competition

1989
Docks Vauban, development plan, Le Havre, France, competition

1989
Restructuring of the "Les Minguettes" district, Venissieux, France, competition

1989
Three towers for offices, residences and hotel, Le Part Dieu, Lyon, France

1989
Transformation of the Casino and enlargement of the Grand Hotel, Cabourg, France, competition

1989
Library, Alexandria, Egypt, competition

1989
Collège 600, Bobigny (Seine-Saint-Denis), France, competition

1989
71 homes, Paola (Cosenza)

1989
Enlargement of the Faculty of Economy and Commerce of the "La Sapienza" University of Rome, Italy

1989
Restructuring of the Louise Michel district, Besancon (Doubs), France, competition

1989
New cemetery, Minturno (Latina), Italy

1989
Restructuring of the Purgatorio, Calamo, Campo-Sportivo, Acri districts (Cosenza), Italy

1989
Motorway control centre, Nances (Savoie), France, competition

1989
Restructuring of the town centre, Bédarieux (Herault) France, competition

1988-1993
Musée des Graffiti, Niaux, France, competition, winning project (with Franco Zagari, Jean Lois Fulcrand, Guy Jordan, Jean Capia)

1988-1989
Layout designing of the "Champ de Mars", Angouleme (Charente), France

1988
Layout designing of the "Jardins de la Fontaine", Nîmes, France, competition with Alain Marguerit, Franco Zagari, Jean Lois Fulcrand, Guy Jordan, Jean Capia

1988
Plant for the transformation of the solid urban waste into methane gas, Nîmes, France, competition, winning project, Jean Lois Fulcrand, Guy Jordan, Jean Capia

1988
Urban plan for the district of the station, Saint-Quentine-en-Yvelines, France, competition, winning project

1988
Restructuring of the town centre, Cergy-Pontoise, France

1988
Layout designing of the "Tiberino" store, Rome, Italy

1988
Tour Bleue, reconstruction, Cergy-Pontoise (Val-d'Oise), France

1988
Chamber of commerce, "Croix Sud", Narbonne (Aude), France with Jean Louis Fulcrand, Guy Giordan, Jean Capia

1988
Triangle de la Folie, Paris-La Défense, France, competition

1988
"West Coast Gateway", Los Angeles (California), United States, competition

1987-1996
Ilot Candie Saint-Bernard, (residences, sports centre, car parks, social and commercial services) for the RIVP, Paris XI, France. Artistic intervention by Enzo Cucchi

1987
Restructuring of the "Anglique-Trois Bornes" residential complex, Saint-Ouen, France, competition

1986-1991
Mediatheque, library, documentation centre, Rezé (Nantes), France

1986-1989
Maison de la Confluence, Avoine, France

1986
European tower: residences, offices, hotel, Herouville-Saint Clair, France, with William Alsop, Jean Nouvel and Otto Steidle

1986
Residences for the Umberto I barracks, layout designing, Orbetello (Grosseto)
1986
Five bus depots for Acotral, Rome, Vitebo, Rieti, Frosinone, Latina, Italy
1986
Studio for artisans, Seuilly (Indre-et-Loire), France
1986
Layout designing of two plazas, sector Raynaldy-Jaurès, Rodez (Aveyron), France, competition
1986
Sculpture park, Orbetello (Grosseto), Italy
1985-1992
New Cemetery, Civita Castellana (Viterbo), Italy
1985-1990
Layout designing and enlargement of Piazza Regina Margherita, Acquappesa, Italy
1985
La Promenade plantée, Bastille-Bois de Vincennes, section Rambouillet, ZAC de Reuilly, 75011, Paris, France, competition
1985
H.L.M. Residences and studios for artists, Seuilly, (Indre-et-Loire), France
1985
Park, Civita Castellana (Viterbo), Italy
1985
Scenography *Attilio Pierelli, Sculptor*, Galleria M.R., Via Garibaldi 53, Rome, Italy
1984-1991
Enlargement of the Cemetery, Orvieto, (Terni) Italy
1984-1991
Spa complex, Cotronei (Catanzaro), Italy
1984-1986
Restructuring and enlargement of a cinema, Cotronei (Catanzaro), Italy
1984-1985
Station, Anagni (Frosinone), Italy
1984
Cemetery, Cotronei (Catanzaro), Italy
1984
Transformation of the covered market into a cultural centre, Civita Castellana (Viterbo), Italy, competition
1984
Conference halls for CIC (Confederation of Italian Growers), in Via M. Fortuny, Rome, Italy, competition
1984
Scenography of the exhibition *De Umbris Idearum* by Giordano Bruno, Palazzo Rivaldi, Rome, Italy
1983-1987
Residential complex, Paliano (Frosinone), Italy

1983
Sport Hall, Sgurgola (Frosinone) Italy, project partially realised
1983
Primary school, Guidonia (Rome), Italy, competition
1983
Economic and Popular Housing Plan, Serrone (Frosinone), Italy
1983
Exhibition: Architectures 1971-1983 School of Architecture Villeneuve-d'Ascq (Lille), France
1982-1990
Casa Serafini, Civita Castellana (Viterbo), Italy
1982
Pavillon Attardi, Fiac, Grand Palais, Paris, France
1982
Parc de la Villette, 75019, Paris, France, international competition
1981-1986
Primary school, Civita Castellana (Viterbo), Italy
1981-1982
Piazza, Cotronei (Catanzaro), Italy
1981
Opéra Bastille, Paris, France, international competition
1980-1990
New headquarters for the Municipal Authority, Cassino (Frosinone), Italy
1980-1984
Sports hall, Rocca di Papa (Rome), Italy
1980-1983
New headquarters for the Municipal Authority, Serrone (Frosinone), Italy
1980
Cultural centre, Cotronei (Catanzaro), Italy
1980
Middle school, Cotronei (Catanzaro), Italy
1980
PRG Serrone (Frosinone), Italy
1979-1986
Sports Complex, Anagni (Frosinone), Italy
1979-1985
Gymnasium, Paliano (Frosinone), Italy
1979-1985
Sports complex, Acute (Frosinone), Italy
1979-1983
Middle school, Cirò Marina (Catanzaro), Italy, with Adriano Pace
1979-1982
Nursery school, Paliano (Frosinone), Italy
1979
New cemetery, Isola del Liri (Frosinone), Italy, competition, winning project

1979
Reconstruction of a district, Turin, Italy
1979
Urban plan PP167, Paliano (Frosinone), Italy
1979
Swimming pool, Fiuggi (Frosinone), Italy
1979
Swimming pool, Piglio (Frosinone), Italy
1978-1988
Middle school "Cava S. Magno", Anagni (Frosinone), Italy
1978
Urban plan PP167, Serrone (Frosinone), Italy
1977-1990
Enlargement of the old cemetery and project for the new cemetery, Paliano (Frosinone), Italy
1977-1984
"Ernica" residential complex, Anagni (Frosinone), Italy
1977-1982
Nursery school and park, Tarquinia (Viterbo), Italy, with the intervention of Sebastian Matta
1977-1980
Residential complex, Anagni (Frosinone), Italy
1977-1979
New cemetery, Acuto (Frosinone), Italy
1977-1979
Urban stairway, Paliano (Frosinone), Italy
1977-1978
Park "Fontana del Diavolo", Paliano (Frosinone), Italy
1977
Urban plan, Serrone (Frosinone), Italy
1977
Park, Sgurgola (Frosinone), Italy
1977
Park, Piglio (Frosinone), Italy
1977
Detailed urban building plan, Pantanello district, Anagni (Frosinone), Italy
1977
Detailed urban building plan, San Filippo district, Anagni (Frosinone), Italy
1977
Urban plan, Tarquinia (Viterbo), Italy
1976-1977
Casa Pilozzi, Acuto (Frosinone), Italy
1976
Business centre, Florence, Italy, competition
1976
Sports complex, Terracina (Latin), Italy
1976
Private house, Farà Sabina (Rieti), Italy
1976
Detailed plan (PP167), Acuto (Frosinone), Italy

1976
Detailed Plan and Popular Housing Plan for the historic centre of Fiuggi (Frosinone), Italy
1975-1986
S. Giorgetto primary school, Anagni (Frosinone), Italy
1975-1979
Restoration and enlargement of a nursery school, Capena (Rome), Italy
1975-1977
Casa Rovaris, Anagni (Frosinone), Italy
1975
Restructuring of two medieval Buildings, Bolsena (Viterbo), Italy
1975
Primary school, Capena (Rome), Italy
1975
Incinerator, Olevano Romano (Rome), Italy
1975
Hotel, Paliano (Frosinone), Italy
1975
Residence, Tomba di Nerone, Rome, Italy
1975
Crusher, Capena (Rome), Italy
1975
Private house, Veroli (Frosinone), Italy
1975
Private house, Campoli Appennino (Frosinone), Italy
1975
Congress centre, Frascati (Rome), Italy
1975
PRG, Acuto (Frosinone), Italy
1974-1975
Restoration and transformation of "Monte Frumentario" into a cultural centre, Via Garibaldi 23, Anagni, (Frosinone), Italy
1974-1975
Restoration of Palazzo Moriconi, Anagni (Frosinone), Italy
1974
Restructuring of Casa Tuffi, Anagni (Frosinone), Italy
1974
Transformation of a hotel from the Liberty period into a hotel school, Fiuggi (Frosinone), Italy
1974
Restoration of a municipal library, Tarquinia (Viterbo), Italy
1974
Tourist residential complex of 650 homes, Palmi (Reggio Calabria), Italy
1974
Skyscraper in the desert, Tunis, Tunisia, competition

1974
School complex (two installations), Anagni (Frosinone), Italy

1974
Tourist centre, Sassocorvaro, (Pesaro Urbino), Italy

1974
Sports complex, Tarquinia (Viterbo), Italy

1974
Incinerator, Anagni (Frosinone), Italy

1973-1983
Residential complex, Esperanza, Via Cartesio 151, Via Nomentana, Rome, Italy

1973
Casa Sacconi, Tarquinia (Viterbo), Italy

1973
Building for two families, Tarquinia-Lido (Viterbo), Italy

1973
Restructuring of Casa Turchiaro, Via Portico d'Ottavia 47, Rome, Italy

1973
House and studio for the sculptor Cascella, Via Aureli, Rome, Italy

1973
Plan for the historic centre of Alatri (Frosinone), Italy, competition

1973
House, Via Appia, Rome, Italy

1973
Swimming pool, Sassocorvaro (Pesaro Urbino), Italy

1973
Road and bridge, Capena (Rome), Italy

1973
Hotel and tourist centre, Rosarno (Reggio Calabria), Italy, with Giovanni Morabito

1973
New type of popular housing, IN-ARCH, Rome, Italy, competition

1972-1975
Residential complex, Monte Livata, Italy, construction not finished by Fuksas

1972-1974
Tourist centre, camping Aurelia, Castel di Guido, Rome, Italy

1972-1973
Restructuring of offices, Rome, Italy

1972-1973
House for 4 families, Bagnaia (Viterbo), Italy

1972
Private house, Tarquinia (Viterbo), Italy

1972
Restructuring of a restaurant-pub-snack bar, Livata (Rome), Italy

1972
Restructuring of the Candeloro offices, Tivoli (Rome), Italy

1972
Holiday resort for winter sports, Monte Livata (Rome), Italy

1972
Cultural centre and plaza, Fiuggi Fonte (Frosinone), Italy

1972
Barracks, Via Salaria, Montelibretti, Rome, Italy

1971-1974
Private residence, Sampalmieri, Via Appia, Rome, Italy

1971
Primary school with 15 classrooms, Tre Fontane, Rome, Italy

1971
Primary school with 10 classrooms, Vigna Murata, Rome, Italy

1971
Layout designing for Private Residence, Maccarelli, Rome, Italy

1971
Vitale Private Residence, EUR, Rome, Italy

1971
Residential centre, Via Aurelia, Rome, Italy

1970-1973
Sport Hall, Sassocorvaro, (Pesaro Urbino), Italy

1970-1972
Private house, Rome, Italy

1970-1971
Landscaping on the area of an old waste dump, San Pancrazio, Tarquinia (Viterbo), Italy

1970-1971
Restructuring private house, Rome, Italy

1970-1971
Landscaping, private property, Rome, Italy

1970
School complex, Pineta Sacchetti, Rome, Italy, competition

1970
Primary school, Casal Bruciato (Rome), Italy

1970
Pavilion of the Province of Rome, Rome Fair, Eur, Rome, Italy

1970
Scenography of an exhibition devoted to satirical-political sketches, with Sebastian Matta (Siné, Wolinsky, Matta, Tim, Pfeiffer, etc), Tarquinia (Viterbo), Italy

1970
Opera House, Belgrade, Yugoslavia, competition

1970
Centre Georges Pompidou, 75003, Paris, France, competition

1969
Flower Market, Pescia (Pistoia), Italy

1968
Scenography of the "Galdos" exhibition, Academy of Spain, San Pietro in Montorio, Rome, Italy

1967
"Galdos" Cultural Centre, Las Palmas de Gran Canaria, Spain, with the sculptor Manolo Bethencourt counter-project

List of collaborators and ex-collaborators
of Fuksas Studio in Rome, Paris and Frankfurt

Lorenzo Accapezzato
Holger Achterholt
Gianluca Adami
Salvatore Addario
Angelo Agostini
Alessia Allegri
Emanuele Altea
Laura Aquili
Francesco Anzolin
Barbara Apolloni
Michele Azzopardi
Chiara Baccarini
Giulio Baiocco
Carmelo Baglivo
Taymoore Balbaa
Fabio Barilari
Athanassios Barkas
Pierpaolo Barone
Narciso Bartellocchi
Ernesto Bartolini
Fabrizio Bastoni
Tobias Baur
Verena Becker
Annalisa Bellettati
Johannes Beherens
Dario Binarelli
Kai Binnewies
Alessio Bonetti
Laura Bonfrate
Elisabetta Biffi
Ralf Bock
Leonardo Brachetta
Tim-Philipp Brendel
Tom Broekaert
Filippo Broggini
Marco Bruschi
Roberta Buccheri
Federico Bucchieri
Maria del Pilar Cabedo
Federica Caccavale
Gianni Cafaggini
Jorge Caminero
Rossana Capurso
Alessandro Carbone
Alessandro Casadei
Angel Casado
Jean-François Casagrande
Sofia Cattinari
Andrea Cavani

Gianluca Centurani
François Champsaur
Irene Ciampi
Giuseppina Ciaramella
Daniel Ciocazanu
Daniela Colli
Paul Collier
Christophe Commenges
Massimiliano Coni
Chiara Costanzelli
Vincent Coste
Riccardo Crespi
Irina Cristea
Michele Cro
Alessandra D'Amico
Gianluca Daga
Vincenzo Daniele
Claudia Dattilo
Alexander De siena
Marco De Bortoli
Adriano De Gioannis
Gianfranco Di Gregorio
Iva Di Pol
Andi Di Vizia
Defne Dilber
Reinhart Dittmann
Aimé Djourno
Andreas Dorrhöfer
Sandra Dotlic
Giorgio Ducci
Marco E Silva
Livia Eusebi
Maria Teresa Facchinetti
Valerie Michele Fanuel
Jean-Michel Fardin
Viorica Feller-Morgan
Serge Filliard
Gabriella Fiorentini
Cristiana Floris
Luca Fornari
Barbara Fragale
Alberto Francini
Petra Frimmel
Marco Frugoni
Wolfgang Gaessler
Riccardo Gaggi
Cristina Gagliardi
Marco Galofaro
Jean-Lucien Gay

Fabrizio Gernei
Francesco Giancola
Cristiana Giovagnoli
Sophie Godet
Enzo Greco
Kathrin Grubert
Fabienne Guedo
Noa Haim
Alexa Hartmann
Tobias Hegemann
Brian Hemsworth
Jan Horst
Klemens Hundertmark
Giuseppe Ippoliti
Allard Jansen
Marina Kavalirek
Kentaro Kimizuka
David Kirwan
Christian Knoll
Matthias Köster
Alexander Kreft
Gianni La Cognata
Luca La Torre
Giampiero Laria La Torre
Davide Leonardi
Julia Lindenthal
Andrea Lupacchini
Giampiero Lustrati
Juan Machado
Susanna Maio Sasso
Guita Maleki
Andrea Marazzi
Davide Marchetti
Juliette Marechal
Simona Martino
Alessandro Mascia
Mario Mattia
Luca Maugeri
Andrew Mckenzie Hull
Martin Mendel
Miguel Mesa
Julien Michel
Ana Milisa
Joost Moolhuijzen
Tiago Mota Saraiva
Massimo Motolese
Maria Motta
Lutz Muerau
Henk Mulder

Katia Necker
Keiko Nogami
Andrea Nolte
Katia Onori
Fabio Oppici
Charles Pailherey
Maurizio Pappalardo
Cesare Pavese
Soren Pedersen
Jamie Peel
Carmen Pena
Luca Peralta
Irène Pham
Luigi Piacentini
Sandi Pirs
Laura Pistoia
Antoine Plazanet
Fiorenza Polacchi
Giancarlo Poli
Carlotta Polo
Also Ponzetti
Luca Punzi
Davide Pavanello
Marco Praturlon
Gijs Pyckevet
Nathalie Quintin
Fabrizio Rafaniello
Steeve Ray
Andrea Ricci
Armando Ricci
Claudio Ronconi
Francesco Rosadini
Delphine Rougé
Pablo Roveran
Ralph Rowekamp
Filomena Russo
Cristiana Saboia
Francesco Sacconi
Takumi Saikawa
Giuseppe Saponaro
Antonio Saracino
Eva Schenck
Concetta Schepis
Matthias Schmidt
Sebastian Schott
Ursula Schuster
Fabio Semprini
Alexis Serikoff
Michael Shevel

Davide Sicilia
Jean-Yann Simmonet
Michael Stahlmann
Kristian Sullivan
Motohiro Takada
Enrico Taranta
Cristiano Tavani
Tasja Tesche
Fang Tiamo
Stefan Tischer
Bertrand Toussaint
Anne Toxey
Daniela Turci
Maria Valencia
Veerie Vanderlinden
Richard Veith
Maria Velez-Ortiz
Matthew Viederman
Assunta Viola
Jens Vogt
Jens Vorbröker
Iain Wadham
Lena Wegener
Santiago Wood
Toyohiko Yamaguchi

Credits

The images come from the Archivio Studio Fuksas, except the following ones:

F. Bat, 72 (1)

Giuseppe Blengini, 208 (4), 212 (9-12), 216 (15-18), 218 (21), 220 (26), 221 (29-30), 225 (41), 227 (44-45)

Gianluca Brancaleone, Andrea Fornello, 249 (3)

Colarossi, 113, 124 (1-2), 140 (4), 146 (2), 147 (4), 156 (2-3)

A. Furudate, 85

Pino Guidolotti, 115 (6-7)

Maurizio Marcato, 188-189, 193, 195, 243 (9-10)

Marchetti, 125

Antonio Martinelli, 73, 77

K. Mattisch, 115 (5)

Christian Meyer, 149, 151 (9-12), 152 (13, 15), 153, 154 (18)

Luca Molinari, 181, 184, 185, 186 (10), 187, 190 (15), 191 (17), 192 (19), 194, 199

Giovanna Piemonti, pag. 62, 63, 64, 65, 67, 68 (3), 69 (5)

Ramon Pratt, 164-165, 224, 225 (40), 237, 238, 239, 240, 241, 242 (7-8)

Philippe Ruault, 129, 130 (6, 7), 131 (8), 133, 134 (13-14), 135 (16), 220 (25)